WHEN COUPLES PART

WHEN COUPLES PART

How the Legal System Can Work for You

by Judge Lawrence E. Kahn

FRANKLIN WATTS
New York/London/Toronto/Sydney/1981

Library of Congress Cataloging in Publication Data

Kahn, Lawrence E   1937–
  When couples part.

  Includes index.
  1. Alimony—United States.   2. Divorce—United
States.   3. Unmarried couples—Legal status, laws,
etc.—United States.   I. Title.
KF537.K33   346.7301′66   80-39821
ISBN 0-531-09944-X

To my precious children
Alyssa, Daniel, and Tamara.

ACKNOWLEDGMENTS

There are many people who have made this book possible. I am much indebted to Carol Schlageter Chady, who did such a wonderful job of editing the drafts of my manuscript, and to Jay Acton, my literary agent and good friend. I am very grateful to Elaine Herkenham, who typed and retyped my manuscript drafts. My deep appreciation must go to Michael Stafford for his wise counsel, to Paul Wein, Michael Daly, Terence Devine, and Pat Maloney, who aided in the legal editing, and to paralegals Marsha Hendry and Tula Mitchell for their research efforts. My editor, Elizabeth Hock of Franklin Watts, put the finishing touches on the book. Most important, special thanks are due to my wife, Michele, whose constant encouragement and incisive editing helped make the book a reality.

Lawrence E. Kahn
February 1981

CAUTIONARY NOTE

Judge Kahn's observations are the result of his experience—ten years as a matrimonial attorney and eight years as a judge. However, as a member of the New York State Judiciary, the author does not in any way intend his writing to reflect how he may decide any issue. Nor is any of his writing intended to provide "crystal ball" legal predictions.

Throughout the book, cases have been created to illustrate a legal point. All of these cases and any names or other facts mentioned therein are purely fictional.

Finally, the only way for the reader to discover his or her legal rights is to seek the advice of an attorney who can best analyze and explain the law as it relates to the reader's personal circumstances.

CONTENTS

Foreword

Chapter 1 ALIMONY   1
         Yesterday
         Today
         Tomorrow
         Wives Caught in the Middle

Chapter 2 MARRIAGE TODAY: A NEW
         DIRECTION   10
         A New Breadwinner in the House
         The Women's Movement
         Wives and Alimony

Chapter 3 THE GUYS GET INTO THE ACT   14
         Alimony for Men
         Dad Can Get Custody, Too
         Joint Custody: Parent Partners

Chapter 4 PALIMONY   25
         A History of Palimony
         The Lee Marvin Case

Where Are We Now?
What to Do If You and Your Friend
Are Pals

Chapter 5   GAYLIMONY   45
              Transalimony

Chapter 6   PREMARITAL CONTRACTS: THE
              DEATH OF ROMANCE?   54

Chapter 7   SEPARATION: THE END OR A NEW
              BEGINNING?   61

Chapter 8   CHOOSING A LAWYER   64
              Peacemaker vs. Killer
              Big Firm vs. Sole Practitioner
              Competent vs. Incompetent
              Matrimonial Expert vs. General
                 Practitioner
              Youth vs. Age
              Should You Hire a Woman Lawyer?
              Establishment Lawyer vs. Maverick
              A Local Attorney vs. an Out-of-Town
                 "Name"
              Do-It-Yourself Divorce: The Fool's Way
              How to Be a Good Client

Chapter 9   DIVORCE: WHOSE FAULT OR NO
              FAULT?   77
              The Effect of No-Fault Divorce on
                 Alimony

Chapter 10   THE DIVORCE BATTLE AND
              ALIMONY   84
              Temporary Divorce Insanity
              Family Court

Chapter 11   ALIMONY: A METHOD TO RESTORE
              ECONOMIC BALANCE   98
              When Alimony Is Not Enough

Alimony Without End
Alimony for Husbands
Some Creative Ways to Make Alimony
 Fair and Useful
Alimony and Child Support: Two
 Separate Issues

Chapter 12   HIDDEN ASSETS   115
             How to Find the Assets

Chapter 13   THE ALIMONY BATTLE AFTER
             DIVORCE   130
             Missing in Action: How to Collect
              Delinquent Alimony Payments
             Lowering the Award
             Increasing the Award
             Remarriage and Alimony
             Enforcement of Court Orders
             Survival Without Alimony

Chapter 14   THE TAX MAN COMETH ALWAYS 147
             Alimony
             Child Support
             Other Tax Considerations

Chapter 15   THE JUDGE   157

Chapter 16   TRENDS   159

             Afterword

Appendix   MAYBE YOU SHOULD MOVE: A
             GUIDE TO THE ALIMONY LAWS
             OF THE FIFTY STATES   164

    Notes   201

    Index   202

Foreword

This book is addressed to people who need courts to work out their financial differences upon the dissolution of their marriage or relationship. While each couple's problems may be unique, there *are* general guidelines to help each and all reach a satisfactory financial arrangement.

My purpose in writing this book is twofold: to provide insight and suggestions, which are intended to help you avoid the shock of a bad decision, the pain of ineffective court procedures, and the frustration of dealing with unsatisfactory lawyers, and to demonstrate that things *can* work out, that the system *does* work, and that it can certainly work for you.

Everyone has heard stories about the woman whom everyone regards with pity because her husband, who earns an impressive salary, dumped her without giving her a cent (leaving her to find a menial job because she was not immediately eligible for anything else) and married his "personal" secretary, or the husband who is stuck with exorbitant alimony payments to an ex-wife who lives with her boyfriend. Unfortunately, these unconscionable situations are not hyperbole; they do exist. However, armed with a better understanding of the legal system, you certainly can increase your chances of being its beneficiary and not its victim.

WHEN COUPLES PART

Chapter 1
ALIMONY

Who invented alimony? The husband's duty to support his wife and her duty to render services to him are two concepts of the common law which date from the time of the Norman Conquest. Upon marriage, a woman lost her legal capacity, especially her property rights. The sacred and traditional concept of marriage was that husband and wife became one, and clearly it was he who was the "one"; the wife became his chattel. In this chauvinistic society, alimony emerged from the unwritten law of England and was allowed at the broad discretion of the ecclesiastical judge. In legal theory, the husband's legal duty to maintain his wife was not ended by the divorce decree. Divorce was only granted to a wife for the most severe kinds of misconduct committed by her husband. When she obtained such a divorce, her request for permanent alimony was usually treated with great sympathy. Early English courts also allowed temporary

1

alimony and counsel fees to defend or prosecute the divorce action. However, such an allowance was almost always smaller than the final permanent alimony award. The amount of alimony was greatly affected by which party was guilty of wrongdoing. An early seventeenth-century definition of alimony was "that allowance which a married woman sues for, upon any occasional separation from her husband; where she is not charged with elopement or adultery."

This temporary alimony was liberally granted because the husband had a duty to support his wife, and this duty continued during the divorce action. There is even an English case in which a wife was allowed temporary alimony even though at the time she was in jail as a convicted felon.[1] In that case, the husband's attorney argued that the wife should be denied temporary alimony, saying she didn't need support because she was being maintained in jail at the expense of the nation. The judge said that was no ground for refusing alimony, but with a quick turn of his legal mind, he directed that the alimony be paid to the Crown while the wife remained in prison.

The main purpose for permanent alimony was to provide the wife with support. The term itself meant maintenance, and it was only allowed if a wife could show that her spouse neglected or refused to make her an allowance suitable to their station in life. The courts would award the wife a fair amount of money and compel the husband to pay it. The factors considered by the court in fixing alimony were the needs of the wife and the financial ability and resources of the husband. The wife was entitled to a "comfortable subsistence in proportion to her husband's income." The wife lost this right to alimony if she was guilty of marital misconduct, such as adultery. The husband's duty to support would only continue for as long as she lived with him or was forced to live apart from him because of his marital wrongdoings. There were no reported cases of a husband receiving alimony. Such an order would have had no legal basis because the wife had no duty to maintain her husband.

William Blackstone's *Commentaries on the Laws of England* discuss in great detail the marital rights of the times. This eighteenth-century classic notes that the laws of England were intended to protect and benefit women. For example, English law liberally provided permanent alimony for a wife upon her receiving a divorce, for the husband's duty to support his wife continued after the termination of the marriage. The same English laws which considered a "man and wife as one person" in some instances considered her separate from him and, in fact, inferior. For example, a wife could not execute a contract nor could she give anything in her will to her husband, for he was supposed to be in total control. Perhaps the most extreme illustration of the inferior status of a woman was that the wife was not held responsible for committing certain kinds of felonies and crimes because she was assumed to have no will of her own and was considered under the constraint of her husband. Blackstone's *Commentaries* concludes with the observation ". . . that even the disabilities, which the wife lies under, are for the most part intended for her protection and benefit. So great a favourite is the female sex of the laws of England." Blackstone would be surprised to discover that the favors of yesterday are considered the insults of today!

The concept of alimony from the common law arrived in this country with the colonists and has survived without any substantial change until the past few decades. Under common law, upon marriage all of a wife's property belonged to her husband outright. Practically speaking, the wife could not even make contracts herself or receive profits from what had been her property. Neither did she get any property rights from her husband. She merged into the marital union and became his! Alimony wasn't awarded to provide justice or retribution but simply as the husband's duty to his wife. The main reason a woman received alimony—no matter how reprehensible the conduct of the man who caused her to seek divorce—was to prevent her from becoming a charge upon the state. Custom and law presumed her destitute because a married woman owned nothing.

In a typical nineteenth-century case, a New York court noted, "Alimony, as we all understand, is an allowance for support and maintenance, having no other purpose and provided for no other object."[2] In another case, a New York court noted in 1843 that it must make in its discretion, "An alimony allowance to a wife for her suitable maintenance and support out of the property of the husband as shall be just and proper. The primary object of alimony is the protection and support of the wife."[3] This same court held that the word "suitable" meant that the wife must not only be maintained and supported but that such support must be appropriate to her station in life.

TODAY

Alimony means many things to many people. To a number of irate husbands, alimony is highway robbery. To feminists, alimony is a vestige of a chauvinistic society which treats a woman in a paternalistic way. To other women, alimony is their means of survival.

It is likely that no one who pays or receives alimony believes it is fair. The man who pays is convinced that he is being taken, and the woman who receives it sincerely believes she is being shortchanged. There is something about alimony—perhaps its connotation of unfairness—which seems to bring out the worst in spouses.

As un-American as it may seem to men, ex-husbands are still sent to jail for not paying alimony. For example, if a court directs a husband to pay $25 a week alimony and he fails to make payments, he may be hauled into a Family Court and directed to pay. If he then fails to obey the Family Court order and pay the arrears, he can be held in contempt for refusing to obey the judge's order and sent to jail. At that time, the judge will not entertain any discussion about the merits and faults of alimony in contemporary society. Nor will there be a great deal of discussion about why it's unfair for him to pay alimony, now that he's remarried with a new family, while his ex-wife is making twice his salary. The judge's prime concern is that this husband did not obey his court order. If court orders are ignored, society would be plunged into chaos. A heavy conclusion to reach over a minor alimony dispute, perhaps, but that's what courts are all about.

It is, therefore, a case of a double bind: The ex-husband has no respect for laws which make him pay his hard-earned money to his not-so-hard-up ex-wife, and the ex-wife has little respect for laws which have no teeth with which to back up a judge's order.

Some states have laws on the books which do not allow a spouse to give up the right to alimony. The public policy of such states is that a husband is obligated to support his wife, and any separation agreement which contains a provision waiving alimony may be void. The theory is that the state has an interest in preserving a family and discouraging divorces.

Many husbands are shocked to discover, as they are taken to court for alimony, that their separation agreement, which was agreeably signed by an ex-wife who "hereby waives all of my rights to support and alimony," was totally void. For example, a husband may agree to pay his wife $200 a week alimony on the condition that if she engages in the same business that he is in within the same city, her right to receive alimony would be suspended. Yet, such a condition would be void in a state which requires alimony because it relieves the husband of his duty to support his wife. His wife could sign this agreement, open a store next door to his business in full competition, and then head over to the courthouse for alimony, and he could not use their separation agreement as a defense. Practically speaking, a judge might be sympathetic to the husband, but legally, the wife would be able to receive alimony despite her agreement to waive it if she went into a competing business near his.

There are other little-known legal facts which make alimony unique. For example, an alimony award cannot be discharged in bankruptcy, and a wife's creditors cannot touch alimony, even for necessaries.

The view held by most states defines alimony as money paid to a wife for a rational and merited reason. It may be money repaid to her or money to restore her to where she would have been if marriage had not diverted her.

When a wife spends twenty years raising the children and caring for the household, freeing her husband to pursue a career, he can't turn around and tell her she's on her own on the day of divorce. She doesn't want favors. All she wants is what she is *owed*—her fair share of the economic worth their marriage has accumulated through the years. In military parlance, her assistance behind the lines was a significant contribution to his work at the front. Part of the prevailing idea is that the wife should be rewarded for years of "sacrifices."

TOMORROW

The laws of alimony are presently in a transitional stage, and a crystal clear definition of "alimony" has yet to emerge. The word itself is so emotionally loaded that acrimony automatically arises when "alimony" is mentioned. If we can substitute a newer and more appropriate phrase, we can better define what alimony really is.

Some terms have been tried but still fall short of serving as an accurate, all-encompassing description of what alimony payments are. "Spousal support" implies that the payments are in the nature of support. Some states use "maintenance," but this implies a duty to "maintain" a dependent spouse. Other states call such payments "rehabilitative" sums, but it seems unfair to imply that a woman who makes a decision to be a homemaker and mother is somehow "disabled" and needs to be "rehabilitated" at the conclusion of this responsible work. Payments made from one spouse to another after divorce should not be alimony, spousal support or maintenance; they should be more in the nature of economic restoration payments. It might be more palatable for a husband, if he was directed by a court to make "restoration payments" to his wife. The word "restoration" even sounds equitable. It would be difficult to find offensive any concept which helps "restore" an economic and self-image balance between divorcing parties. A Motion for Restoration in court would place the burden on the one seeking such payments to prove that he or she was treated in a manner which requires payment to fairly settle the economic aspects of the marriage. A wife in such a position is not asking her ex-husband for a handout: she's demanding what is hers.

Many states still protect an ex-wife's right to support but don't recognize her share of the marital property. This attitude is slowly changing in all fifty states. The new concept of alimony is taking hold—specifically, a money payment made by one spouse to another designed to balance and equalize any economic loss sustained as a result of their marital relationship. The historic use of alimony as a form of punishment or revenge upon an errant husband, or for the purpose of supporting an estranged wife, is slowly fading from the law.

And alimony is falling into more disrepute as wives become less economically dependent on their husbands. Equal opportunities, women's rights, two-income families, the growth of day care facilities, and other changes in today's society leave less and less sympathy for the woman who still needs financial help when her marriage fails.

WIVES CAUGHT IN THE MIDDLE

Despite these liberating trends, contemporary American society still has millions of women, particularly between the ages of forty and sixty, who require economic help from their husbands when divorce occurs. The new attitudes and climate which foster the independent woman make it even harder for these wives who do need help. The switch from chauvinistic attitudes, on the bench and in the law, to just determinations not based on sex or gender have caught many wives in a bind. Some women feel guilt or shame in seeking alimony. The pendulum is swinging from wives who receive alimony for no valid reason to wives who are not given reasonable financial help when they need and deserve it. A woman born in the 1920s, '30s, and early '40s, raised to believe that a woman's place was not in the work force but in a home raising children, may find herself out of place or at least uncomfortable with some aspects of the '70s and '80s. When divorce strikes, she finds herself unwanted and unready for the new world. True, she is aware of the struggle for women's rights and she may even admire her own daughter's independent spirit. But her daughter had the benefit of growing up in a different time with different peers. The bottom line is a wife who is not emotionally or educationally equipped to make it on her own. For her, plain, old-fashioned alimony is still necessary.

Yet, the end of alimony as we presently know it is in sight. The purpose and need are changing as the roles of both father and mother drastically change within the family. With the breakdown of role distinctions and with increased equality between the sexes, both in and out of marriage, alimony is often no longer a primary concern between divorcing parties. In time, it will be an historical oddity.

Chapter 2
MARRIAGE TODAY: A NEW DIRECTION

Many wives still live in traditional home environments where the husband is dominant and family life revolves around him. That is their business. Fulfillment comes in many ways; in other words, different strokes for different folks.

The traditional relationship between male and female is being tested severely by massive changes in attitude. As a woman seeks her own fulfillment, self-sufficiency, and independence, the interaction between her and her husband changes. The man may feel less needed as his wife is more able to protect and care for herself, and she, in turn, may feel less *in need*. This will inevitably affect their marital relationship; as their respective needs change, so will there be a risk that the marriage will have less purpose for remaining intact.

A NEW BREADWINNER
IN THE HOUSE

The most significant change within family life in the past two decades is the dramatic increase in the number of wives who work outside the home. The traditional concept of the husband as breadwinner and the wife as homemaker is no longer realistic. Inflation, women's rights, and the great number of single-parent homes are pushing more and more women into the work force. While there are many factors, a major reason for both husband and wife to work is the economy. It's a matter of survival. One breadwinner per house is no longer enough. Making ends meet is particularly difficult in light of the burgeoning divorce and remarriage rates and the burden of supporting two families, for it has gotten to the point where it takes two incomes to meet even the basic needs of one family in America today. Just as our economy demands that both husband and wife share the income-producing role for their family, so too will it help reduce the demand for alimony payments when such a marriage ends.

THE WOMEN'S MOVEMENT

The Women's Movement need not necessarily conflict with a strong family unit in today's society. But it has altered the traditional concept of family. Women have the choice of living within the context of a family, rejecting it to compete in the outside world, or doing both.

The thrust of the Women's Movement is simply that every woman has the right to do anything that a man does and should have equal opportunity to make any such choice. Of course, among the options are marriage, raising children, and running a household. The woman who so chooses may be happier than one who has the same responsibilities but is forced by economic necessity to work. The latter may have a liberated attitude, but she also may be extremely frustrated because she feels guilty that she is not with her children and keeping her home as she feels she must in order to be a good mother and wife.

Despite pressure from the Women's Movement, entrenched values still persist in American "justice." While logic or theory may dictate that a mother and father should be viewed equally in a custody dispute, there are those who still strongly believe that a mother's love automatically surpasses that of a father, and the woman, therefore, has the edge over the man in court. Prevailing attitudes of a male-dominated society sustain many double standards for family life. Society still views a woman adultress with greater horror than an unfaithful man. Many judges still believe that a red-blooded American male is supposed to work, and that the woman belongs in the house—and they do not mean the House of Representatives! With regard to divorce, these same judges feel that the ex-husband is supposed to keep working to support his family and the ex-wife is supposed to remain a dutiful mother. Even today, a man who refuses to work can be put in jail for not paying support, while the wife who refuses to work is more apt to receive alimony.

WIVES AND ALIMONY

A significant number of wives today refuse to request alimony. Many a wife finds it demeaning to ask a court to make her husband give weekly stipends after divorce.

Her attitude comes through loud and clear: she doesn't need him to "make it." She managed well without him before they were married, and she'll be better off without him when the marriage is over. Such a liberated wife certainly expects her husband to equally share the responsibility of raising their children—that's only fair. But once their marriage is over, their responsibility to each other is also ended. True, there will be financial problems to work out. Some form of property settlement is unavoidable because assets accumulated during the marriage have to be sorted out and divided fairly. But as for alimony itself, the concept has no place.

Many additional pressing contemporary issues will help force alimony out of the judicial limelight. The needs of society are continually changing, and law grows and molds itself around new challenges. Living out of wedlock, "illegitimate" children, pre-marriage contracts, post-nuptial agreements, and term marriages may all become the new concerns of our courts though, in fact, none of these is really new. A self-congratulatory younger generation is apt to think they are the first to live together without getting married; well they might, for they have no recollection of their great uncle and aunt who did the same thing under the respectable guise of common-law marriage! And so the marriage wheel turns. . . .

Chapter 3
THE GUYS GET INTO THE ACT

ALIMONY FOR MEN

Historically, alimony was not for husbands. A wife did not owe her husband a duty of support because it was he who did the supporting. By 1886 only two states had laws allowing alimony for husbands. By the 1930s approximately fifteen states had such statutes. And by 1979 only ten states had laws which limited alimony to wives: Alabama, Arkansas, Georgia, Idaho, Mississippi, New York, South Carolina, South Dakota, Tennessee, and Wyoming. Finally, this ancient concept of wives-only alimony was ended by the United States Supreme Court in a 1979 landmark decision.[4] The court held an Alabama alimony law unconstitutional, saying the law which provided alimony for a wife and not for a husband violated the equal protection clause. The court specifically stated that state law should "treat men and women equally by making alimony burdens independent of sex." The United States Supreme Court concluded that the Ala-

14

bama statute carried with it "the baggage of sexual stereotypes," and further that "the state cannot be permitted to classify on the basis of sex."

The United States Supreme Court was telling all states to treat a husband and wife equally when legislating any form of spousal support. The decision did away with the historical basis of alimony: a husband's duty to support his wife. Now each state can take a fresh look at its alimony laws and consider the underlying purpose of spousal support.

This recent decision supports egalitarian principles and contemporary values. It also reflects the economic realities that now exist. More than half the country's married women work outside the home. No longer is it uncommon to find a wife who earns more than her husband. This fact alone has significant effects on alimony determinations throughout America's courtrooms.

LES AND MARCIA SNYDER

Les and Marcia Snyder were not only well-suited marriage partners but also excellent business partners. When they first got married, they opened a small motel and over the years expanded the business until, after 22 years, they were running a highly successful dude ranch-motel resort. Les was the nice guy who kept the guests happy. He was always able to work out any disputes among guests or employees. When a tough job had to be handled, Marcia played the "bad guy." She found it easy because she *was* tough. In fact, they would never have done well without Marcia's push and business acumen. She was the strong one with the good business mind. If matters had been left to Les, everyone would have had a great time, but the business would have long since gone bankrupt. Marcia recognized his limitations and her own abilities. She kept a strong control over the motel and ranch. Les didn't mind because he knew that he could never equal Marcia's talent in that department. Marcia found it easy to say "No" or "You're fired"; he never could.

Marcia did have one fault. While it was easy for her to nix anything in the business world, she could never say no to an attractive man. Perhaps that's why Marcia always kept her finger on personnel matters, including hiring and firing. There wasn't a busboy, lifeguard, or stablehand she hadn't personally selected. She gave them experience—on the job and off. Perhaps Les knew about his wife's "weakness," but he always looked the other way.

When Marcia reached age 48, she suddenly turned on Les. Some thought it was because of menopause; others thought it was because their only child, Chad, had moved to the West Coast, removing any tempering influence he might have provided while at the ranch. Whatever the reason, Marcia began treating Les with disdain and outright cruelty. Her public degrading of Les humiliated him until he took the only action which fitted his personality—he packed his bags and walked out. Considerably later, when he was served with divorce papers, he had no choice but to go to a lawyer. It was only then that he found how badly he had been treated financially. His lawyer showed him that their once modest motel was now a thriving business enterprise with a net worth of approximately $450,000. Until the lawyer said so, it never even occurred to Les that he might be able to receive alimony from Marcia. He had supported himself by working at odd jobs for a few bucks at a time, while Marcia raked in the profits at the ranch.

By the time all of the financial intricacies of their business were sorted out in the divorce action, it was clear that Marcia had taken advantage of her position as business manager throughout the years by hoarding all the profits for herself. She had invested the annual net profits in stocks and bonds in her own name. She had also purchased real estate and apartment houses in a nearby city, again in her own name. Les's lawyer attempted to convince the court that all these monies were accumulated as a joint enterprise, and Les, as Marcia's business partner, was entitled to an equal share of the worth accumulated during the marriage.

The judge awarded Les alimony of $200 a week. He based this award on Marcia's substantial earnings compared to Les's meager income and his obvious inability to provide well for himself. Outsiders thought it ludicrous that Les was receiving alimony. Those who knew the facts of the case thought the decision left Les shortchanged.

In time, such cases may become more common as husbands' and wives' roles become more interchangeable.

DAD CAN GET CUSTODY, TOO

The classic stereotypes are mom as nurturer, caring intensely for every need of her child, and dad as detached and macho provider, throwing kisses to his daughter and

17

playing ball with his son. It was expected that after divorce the mother would keep the child, and the father would visit periodically. Certainly he could fill his limited role in the space of a Sunday afternoon.

Now, with lifestyles changing so rapidly, we find less distinction between the roles of mother and father in the typical family unit. Both parents often work and, with the expansion of women's rights, both father and mother have greater equality in dealing with one another and their children. These new attitudes have altered their roles as mother and father to their children. No longer is it unusual or unmasculine for a father to be extremely attached to his children. And with the greater involvement of fathers there comes an increase in the number who go to pieces when they find they may lose custody of their children in a divorce proceeding. On the other side of the coin, society is less appalled than it once was when a mother willingly turns over custody to the father, so she can have the freedom to pursue her own career, or perhaps because she admits her husband can take better care of the children than she can.

The husband is now often willing to contest the custody issue. It wasn't so long ago that this was virtually unheard of, not to mention their winning such cases! Fathers' rights have greatly increased during the past decade and the Women's Movement deserves most of the credit. When the Equal Rights Amendment, women's lib, and equal opportunity drives came along, courts were forced for the first time to look at a woman without regard to sex. As soon as the courts did this, their attention was called to the fact that many laws discriminated against the man in favor of the woman. For example, when a child was born out of wedlock, the mother had all rights to the child, and the father had none. Even today, many states have laws which permit the mother of an out-of-wedlock child to surrender the child for adoption without even consulting the father. Nor do these laws require his consent. Some recent decisions have overturned these laws in an attempt to give equal rights to the father.

Nowhere has the impact of the Women's Movement been felt more greatly than in custody disputes. For years, most courts gave great weight to the "tender years" doctrine which recognized mother love as essential to the well-being of an infant. Because of this attitude, the courts viewed a mother's rights as superior to the father's during the early or "tender" years of infancy. Until recently, it was simply accepted without contest that a child under age three was better off with the mother than with the father. As fathers now move into an active role of parenting, as mothers move away from such a role by seeking employment, and as husband and wife view each other equally in light of recent trends in both law and society, doctrines which prefer one sex over the other solely on the basis of gender are becoming less valid. Thus is the "tender years" doctrine slowly being eroded. Courts are now starting to look at the husband and wife as equals in their parental roles. Judges are issuing fewer decisions with such statements as, "The mother is the preferred custodian for young children," or, as a New York judge stated only a few years ago, "The law of nature requires that the child should be reared by its mother, the one who has borne the agony of childbirth, and upon whom has fallen the care and vigil and trouble of nurturing and caring for her offspring."[5] Today, more fathers win custody of their children. No longer does one view with shock a father who has custody of his children, nor does his having custody imply that the mother abandoned the family or is in some other way a despicable parent. As courts begin to view mother and father in an equal light, more and more fathers will find themselves victors in custody disputes. This is not to suggest that the pendulum will swing to favor fathers, but only that a father who truly wants custody of his children will at least have a chance. In the past, a custody battle often meant a waste of time and money with no possibility of success for a father, no matter how much the facts favored his position. A series of recent cases have even recognized the rights of unwed fathers, as judges now are more inclined to base their decisions on the best interest of the child. This equal treatment under law will also have an impact on alimony disputes. By placing mother and father on equal footing in a custody battle, the courts may be more prone to view parents on an equal economic footing.

But despite tremendous changes in law, there still remains a strong prejudice in favor of a mother in a custody dispute, and it is still the exception when a father gets the child. Many divorces begin with one spouse leaving the house, and it is usually the man who goes. When he leaves, it's expected that he take his shirt, pants, socks, shoes, briefcase, camera, and a few other personal items essential to his survival. But let him lay a finger on the lawn mower, his workbench, tools, or other such property and the battle begins. The biggest battle often is over the stereo! No other item causes more friction, endless litigation, and vicious behavior. That is, except for the children. It would be unthinkable for a husband to turn to his wife and say, "Honey, we just can't keep up this sham any longer; it's time we split. I'm leaving this weekend, and I'm taking all of my clothes, personal papers, and the children." But if a wife says to her husband, "I know we've tried to make it, but it's just not working; I'm leaving tomorrow to go live with my parents, and I'm taking my clothes, the china and silverware, and the children," not one eyebrow would be raised. While the Women's Movement has greatly enhanced the rights of men, the fact remains that in any custody battle the woman still has an edge over her husband, and the younger the children, the greater the edge.

JOINT CUSTODY: PARENT PARTNERS

One legal trend is the increasing use of joint custody. In terms of legal rights and obligations, joint custody is still a vague and undefined area which could lead to more problems than it solves. Joint custody merely states that the child remains in the custody of both parents, although the parents live apart. Of course, the child can reside in only one home, but a joint custodial arrangement envisions the child having greater opportunity to live with each parent whenever circumstances allow. More important, joint custody implies that decisions regarding the child—medical treatment, schooling, or other matters in the upbringing—will be shared by the parents. There's no question that such an arrangement is geared to benefit child and parents.

In some ways, winning custody serves as a sort of catharsis to the victor, for he or she feels vindicated and less guilty over the marriage failure. After all, when you walk away from a marriage with the most valuable assets of the relationship—the offspring—it is easier to believe that you are "the good half."

Clearly, the worst part of awarding one parent custody and the other visitation is that the children are dragged into the divorce proceeding. Divorce always has a traumatic effect on children, and bringing them into the fray can be devastating. In too many proceedings, children have been used as the pawns of battling parents. By tactics such as brainwashing (the better to hurt the other parent) children are abused during divorce.

21

Joint custody, although still unusual, actually views divorce exactly as it is—a split between spouses, not a split between parents and children. It encompasses much more than physical custody of the child. In a joint custody arrangement, the parent having physical custody of the child is obliged to consult the other parent about major decisions relating to the child. Such decisions could include the child's medical needs, schooling, religious training, extracurricular programs, summer camps, and similar activities which substantially bear on growth and development. More important than these aspects, however, are the psychological and emotional advantages of joint custody. Joint custody means that while mom and dad may no longer love each other, they both still want to share parenting. It also means that while mom and dad no longer live together, both will make it their business to continue to share concern and responsibility for raising their children. Furthermore, it means that both parents recognize each other as equals in responsibility for raising their children. They no longer are marriage partners, but they remain parent partners.

It's not always easy to make joint custody work. Many times a woman finds it galling that her ex-husband who, in her eyes was not only a bad husband but a lousy father, *now* takes the time to call frequently, offer parental advice, and assert his fatherly concern. Nevertheless, the fact is that it's better for the kids that their father has this new-found interest in them. Some women would prefer that their ex-husbands take off and ignore the kids so *they* can spend the remaining years bemoaning their fate and telling the children what a stinker their father was. This may bolster her morale, but it wreaks havoc on her children's psyches. A child's own chance for happiness is quite slim when a mother continually harps on an evil father who abandoned the family.

Joint custody encourages both parents to take an

active interest in their children and minimizes the trauma dealt a child in the standard custody situation, where she tends to feel loved by one parent and abandoned by the other. A child's mental health will be much better for his knowing that both parents are still jointly responsible for him. Likewise, the mental health of both parents should also be better for their knowing that they are still parents—even if they are "failures" at marriage. For example, a father with joint custody finds it much more palatable to meet his support obligations and more fulfilling to communicate with his children when he knows that he is equally responsible for their upbringing.

It might not be long before all divorces, with few exceptions, will automatically include a joint custody award. The standard divorce might then state, "It is hereby ordered, adjudged, and decreed that the children of the marriage will be in the joint custody of both plaintiff mother and defendant father, with the children to reside with the plaintiff mother throughout the year, except for alternate weekends, one week during the winter vacation, one week during the spring vacation, and one month during the summer vacation during which time they shall reside with defendant father."

A joint custody award obviously cannot perpetuate the same kind of living arrangements enjoyed during marriage. Although custody is joint, the child will basically live with one parent throughout the year for purposes of stability. So in a sense, the physical living arrangements for the child do not differ much whether there is joint custody or the traditional one parent custody–one parent visitation arrangement. The significant differences lie in the attitudes of the parents toward each other and toward their children, as well as the child's view of his parents and of himself.

Finally, the very mentality which accepts joint custody usually rejects the concept of alimony. A divorcing couple who view each other as having equal and joint responsibility in raising their children will most usually view each other as being equal, independent individuals. A wife who agrees to joint custody will feel secure enough not to be threatened by sharing control of "her" children equally with her former husband. She won't be out to prove anything and she won't feel the need to cling to the children as her own personal possessions—permitting her husband only limited and controlled visits. If she views herself and her husband in this healthy light, then the odds are that she will not want financial support for herself.

Chapter 4
PALIMONY

As much as society and its mores change, one thing remains constant: people want to have their cake and eat it too. Now the courts are faced with the girlfriend who asks for support after she has been rejected by her boyfriend. The idea behind this form of alimony—or "palimony" as it is now labeled—is that when two people live together, they have a special relationship which is significantly different from the way each lived before. When the arrangement ends, some repayment or compensation may be warranted to restore any unfair economic imbalance or loss. If a man and woman share the same home for three, four, or twenty-five years, shouldn't they receive the same consideration and treatment by the courts that married couples receive when they split up? True, a marriage is a binding agreement, a contract which carries certain legal duties, obligations, and privileges. However, the counterargument is that if equity and justice warrant an award of money to a married woman who has given ten years of her life to her husband, paid his way through school, and helped him start a prosperous business, then why shouldn't the unmarried woman who has done the same be entitled to the same equity and justice?

Of course, it could be argued that if palimony is awarded to people who have lived together without marrying, such relationships may ultimately be discouraged; hence the need for palimony will abate. One advantage of living together without a marriage commitment is there are no legal ties or obligations, but the advent of palimony has changed all of that.

"Lee Marvin" cases are now popping up all over the country and are symptomatic of a society in which more and more people are living together without the benefit of a marriage license. In the past decade, the number of unmarried couples living together has doubled, and one third of these couples are forty-five and older. Obviously, this new lifestyle has not been pre-empted by the younger generation. Why? Not long ago one of America's favorite songs went "Love and marriage, love and marriage, go together like a horse and carriage." Today, the horse is unhitched! Today, those who don't see marriage as flexible are afraid of it. Others are afraid of a marriage relationship because they've already been hurt by one. Rather than immediately enter into a new, binding commitment, they prefer to test the relationship first. In this way, they can avoid or at least postpone the risks of a bad marriage—namely, a traumatic divorce and all of the legal hoopla that goes along with it (including such frightening obligations as alimony).

No age group or particular generation has cornered the market on living out of wedlock. It's not at all unusual to find an elderly couple in their eighties walking hand in hand along the beaches of Miami, sharing love without marriage. They, as so many couples of all ages, join together to end loneliness and to share a fulfilling life together—and one which still allows them both to receive full Social Security or tax benefits, which would be decreased if they marry. It is ironic, but it *may* be more economically advantageous for senior citizens to live together.

Precisely because there is no binding commitment, unmarried couples may face the prospect of a parting of ways to a higher degree than married couples. When such a couple does break up, they more often than not go their own ways without seeking anything from each other, but the question of support and division of property may arise. Often, such relationships are entered without deep commitments or long-term expectations, nor is there usually reliance which would warrant settlement when the relationship ends. Nevertheless, when two people live together for a significant period of time during which various commitments arise, a break-up can be expected to be more momentous and painful than one involving people who have only the usual, brief sleep-in arrangements. It may be that the deeper the hurt, the more need there is to seek legal redress.

Most courts have not recognized the same kinds of rights for unmarried couples as they give married ones. Living together without the benefit of a marriage contract is a statement to society that a couple is not going to follow the restrictive values imposed by society. Theoretically, a couple should not have to get a license to love; it's no one's business, and especially not the business of our bureaucratic government. But people in such relationships cannot then turn around when they're in trouble and ask for rules, governmental interference, and courts to help them when things don't work out. Or can they? Why shouldn't they be able to seek legal help if they need it?

The stated public policy of most states is to encourage and preserve family structure. Such a family unit is based on marriage vows and legal commitments made between the marriage partners. The power of government strongly backs every rule, regulation, and law which strengthens anything that legally binds together a married couple. As a significant by-product of this public policy, thousands of government clerks throughout our nation are kept busy keeping records of marriage licenses, births, divorces.

Hand in hand with this attitude of backing legitimate marital relationships goes the thought that little should be done to confer legal recognition on the living arrangements of unmarried couples. Most state laws do not give inheritance rights to children born out of wedlock. The federal government will not give Social Security benefits to surviving unmarried "spouses." Courts generally have a hands-off policy for battling, unmarried couples. Many other governmental and legal resources are denied unmarried couples, perhaps in the hope that someday they'll capitulate and get married. While the institution of matrimony has not had any great record of success in recent decades, it is still favored over all alternatives. Thus, palimony has not fared well in American law.

A HISTORY OF PALIMONY

Palimony cases are not new to the twentieth century. Couples living together outside of marriage have a long and splendid history both in and out of court.

As early as 1885, a Kansas case held that in all judicial separations of unmarried persons who have lived together as husband and wife, "a fair and equitable division of their property should be had."[6] In making its decision, the Kansas court inquired into the amount each party originally owned, the amount each received while

28

living together, and the amount of joint accumulations, and then gave the woman half the property. And in 1892, a New York court held that when a man and woman live together for thirty-two years during which time the woman kept house and cooked and worked on the farm, there was sufficient evidence of an expressed contract between them to warrant her receiving an award for services rendered.[7] This New York court held that there was evidence that the woman was of great assistance to the man and was worth certainly as much as "an ordinary hired man," and also that he had intended to pay her for her services and to will his farm to her. Most important, the court noted that the illicit relations of the parties did not necessarily forbid an expressed contract between them. Of course, most courts were not that prescient in the Gay Nineties. In another New York case, only six years later, the court held that where a man and woman agree to live together and also enter into a co-partnership to mutually pool their financial resources in a common fund, such a contract would not be recognized by the courts.[8] The judge noted indignantly, "It is difficult to imagine a more audacious challenge to a court of justice for the enforcement of an immoral contract than that which appears in this complaint." The judge observed that the case contained no facts which showed a "condition as arises when a young girl, ignorant and unfamiliar with the wiles of men, is deceived and betrayed into an illicit union, where a court might sometimes be astute in seeking methods to avoid injustice. The present action is that of a widow whose eyes may be supposed to have been opened by a previous taste of the fruits of the tree of knowledge of good and evil, who now alleges that she had contracted with defendant to enter into a state of concubinage, asking a court of equity to sanction the contract and award her the price of her shame."

In an even earlier case, a Louisiana court in 1852

held that a man and woman who lived together as man and wife cannot acquire rights to each other's property.[9] The court said that, "A participator in concubinage is incapable of recovering, as a universal partner, one half of property acquired." However, this nineteenth-century Louisiana case contained a "twentieth-century" dissenting opinion which failed to convince the majority court that any two people who live together and contribute capital in labor within the relationship should be entitled under the laws of equity to one half of the property they accumulate. That judge stated that, "if both parties had been men or both women, they would fully establish a partnership between them."

As far back as 1825, a New York case dealt with an extramarital affair where a young woman lived with a man in an illicit relationship during which time she bore him two children.[10] The man had promised to continue to support the woman in the event that they broke up, and the court once again grappled with the difficult issue of immorality while attempting to deal fairly with a young woman who may have been taken advantage of. The court could not reach any conclusion in this case and instead decided that there was not enough evidence shown which would make a support contract void. The judge refused to decide the case without further evidence, since they couldn't decide if the contract was made for the "purpose of facilitating a continued prostitution," or was "a contract apart from such an immoral agreement."

A number of cases in this century also hold that when a man and woman live together without the benefit of marriage, they are entitled to share in the assets accumulated during the relationship, at least to the extent that they each contributed financial resources which produced economic benefit. The main concern of each court is to separate the extramarital conduct from the financial relationship of the couple. A number of California cases have held that an agreement made between a man and woman who also live together may be enforced to the extent that the agreement deals with their property and business rights. But such an agreement must be totally unrelated to their extramarital relationship. In one California case, the court held that, where a man and woman lived together and had agreed to combine their assets and earnings to acquire property, the property was to be divided equally between them at the time they broke up, pursuant to their earlier agreement.[11] Another California court held that a woman is entitled to share property jointly accumulated while she lives with a man to the extent that her funds contributed to the acquisition of the property.[12] In a 1932 case, a California court held that an agreement between an unmarried man and woman who lived together, which stated that each would invest in property for their mutual benefit with each having an undivided half interest, was an enforceable contract.[13] The court rejected the man's contention that the contract was void since their relationship had been illicit. The court simply found that the agreement to split their property, while made at the same time as their agreement to live together, was a separate and distinct matter. As early as 1908, a California case held that permanent alimony could not be granted even when the woman helped to acquire and materially add to her boyfriend's property. Yet the court did allow her a substantial allowance to compensate her for the benefits derived by her unmarried mate during their relationship.[14]

Courts often strain to find just and equitable results. Legal contortions are not unusual when a court tries to do "the right thing." These judicial attempts at fairness go just so far, and lines are drawn so the status of the law is maintained. The result is a greater abundance of cases in all states which deny any form of payment to a woman who lives with a man in a state of unmatrimony. In a 1943 case, a California court held that a woman was not entitled to support from a man she lived with merely because they lived together, and such an illicit relationship could not confer any financial benefits.[15] This case did have a dissenting opinion which urged the majority court to recognize an implied agreement between the couple to share their property. This lone judge felt that the majority court punished the woman for her part in the illicit relationship and placed no value on her services as a cook, housekeeper, and homemaker. This minority opinion noted that the man was an equally guilty party in the extramarital relationship and was able to go out and work to earn money to purchase property only because of his girlfriend's services. This approach did not sway the California court in 1943, and it would continue to fail to convince most American courts today, despite some inroads to the contrary.

Courts are particularly wary of a contract which attempts to stymie marriage. For instance, under the California Civil Code, every contract in "restraint of marriage" is void. So a 1942 California case held an oral contract void in which a divorced woman agreed to forgo marrying any other person and contracted to accept employment with a married man.[16] Besides agreeing not to marry, the woman agreed to be the man's lifelong companion and maintain a home for him in return for his supporting her for the remainder of her life. The woman carried out her part of the agreement for more than seventeen years when suddenly the man stopped supporting her. She went to court to enforce her contract, but the court backed him and held that he had no obligation to support her because their contract "in restraint of marriage" was void. The court also stated that the contract was not lawful, since it was "contrary to good morals."

Besides California, many other states have had to grapple with these palimony issues. In a 1950 New York case involving a man and woman who lived together for twenty years, during which time each contributed to the purchase of land, the court held that there was sufficient evidence to prove an oral agreement for common ownership of the property.[17] The agreement was considered implied and with each party owning half interest in the land. In another 1950 case, a Kentucky court leaned more strongly to "moral" considerations and held that the fact that a man and woman lived together for many years did not entitle either of them to any economic benefits accrued during the relationship.[18] This Kentucky court noted that the woman, who was seeking her interest in land that she had conveyed to her long-time, live-in boyfriend, was already married when she entered into a bigamous marriage with this man, and being guilty of bigamy, she was not entitled to any help from the court. Puerto Rico also has had to deal with these moral issues. In 1927 a Puerto Rican court held that a woman who lived with a man for more than forty years and helped him accumulate property during that time was not entitled to any share of this property because "Concubinage was the cause and reason of their living together at his house, and cooperation and work which she rendered there were incidental to her relationship as a concubine."[19]

THE LEE MARVIN CASE

All of the above-mentioned cases constituted the legal background for the 1970's Lee Marvin case which sent shock waves across America.[20] This case was really no different from many others throughout the United States

33

in the past two hundred years, except for the glare of the news media focused on the famous couple: Actor Lee Marvin and Michelle Triola Marvin. (Though she used his last name, she had never been married to him.)

In the very first sentence of its decision, the California Supreme Court noted that there has been a substantial increase in the number of couples living together without the benefit of marriage. Lee Marvin and Michelle Triola Marvin had lived together for seven years without marrying, and during that time all of their property was acquired in Lee Marvin's name alone. Michelle Triola Marvin alleged in her action that she and Lee Marvin had "entered into an oral agreement," that while "the parties lived together they would combine their efforts and earnings and would share equally any and all property accumulated as a result of their efforts." Ms. Triola also alleged that she and Lee Marvin had agreed to "hold themselves out to the general public as husband and wife," and that "she would further render her services as a companion, homemaker, housekeeper, and cook to him." According to Ms. Triola, the crux of their agreement was that she was to "give up her lucrative career as an entertainer and singer" in order to "devote her full time to Lee Marvin . . . as a companion, homemaker, housekeeper, and cook"; in return for which, Mr. Marvin agreed to "provide for all of her financial support and needs for the rest of her life." Ms. Triola did live with Lee Marvin from October of 1964 through May of 1970, and she allegedly fulfilled her obligations under the alleged oral agreement. The court noted that, "during this period, the parties as a result of their efforts and earnings acquired, in defendant Lee Marvin's name, substantial real and personal property, including motion picture rights worth over one million dollars." In May of 1970, Lee Marvin compelled Michelle Triola Marvin to leave his household, although he did continue to support her until

34

November 1971. Based on these facts, Ms. Triola brought her action, claiming that the oral contract entitled her to share the property acquired when she and Lee Marvin lived together.

Lee Marvin's main contention was that the alleged oral contract was so closely related to the "immoral" character of their relationship that it would violate public policy if it were enforced. The California court did not buy this argument and specifically held that "the fact that a man and woman live together without marriage, and engage in a sexual relationship, does not in itself invalidate agreements between them relating to their earnings, property, or expenses." The court's opinion was based on the principle that "adults who voluntarily live together and engage in sexual relations are nonetheless as competent as any other persons to contract respecting their earnings and property rights." The court was careful to point out that a couple "cannot lawfully contract to pay for the performance of sexual services, for such a contract is, in essence, an agreement for prostitution and unlawful for that reason." But the court then went on to say that an unmarried couple "may agree to pool their earnings and to hold all property acquired during the relationship in accord with the law governing community property." In essence, the California court said that as long as the agreement itself does not rest upon the "illicit . . . consideration," a couple may arrange their economic affairs as they choose.

This California court also rejected the theory of "punishing" a "guilty" partner. In other words, the court would not throw out an unmarried woman seeking equitable economic relief merely because she engaged in an illicit affair, and thus came to court as an "immoral" or "guilty" party. The court specifically noted that if it were to deny relief in order to punish the unmarried woman, it necessarily would follow that it would be rewarding the other partner by permitting him to retain a disproportionate amount of the property which might rightfully belong to her. The court specifically stated that, "concepts of 'guilt' thus cannot justify an unequal division of property between two equally 'guilty' persons." In other words, the court said that each of the unmarried partners was equally responsible for their living arrangement and illicit relationship, and therefore both would be treated equally in court.

The court also rejected the contention that by opening up the courts to nonmarital partners, it would be discouraging marriage. The court noted that it certainly supported the well-established public policy to promote marriage; however, "perpetuation of judicial rules which result in an inequitable distribution of property accumulated during a nonmarital relationship is neither a just nor an effective way of carrying out that policy." The California court then went on to discuss the "prevalence of nonmarital relationships in modern society and the social acceptance of them." The court stated that "we are aware that many young couples live today without the solemnization of marriage, in order to make sure that they can successfully later undertake marriage. This trial period, preliminary to marriage, serves as some assurance that the marriage will not subsequently end in dissolution to the harm of both partners." In effect, this court was recognizing that the mores and values of society have changed radically in recent years in regard to cohabitation without marriage, and because of these drastic changes, the court refused to "impose a standard based on alleged moral considerations that have apparently been so widely abandoned by so many." Because of these new mores, the court concluded that "judicial barriers" should no longer stand in the way of providing equitable and legal relief for a nonmarital relationship.

At the very end of its decision, this California court

thought it wise to give a belated cheer for the institution of marriage. "Lest we be misunderstood," the court went on to praise marriage and noted that the "structure of society itself largely depends upon the institution of marriage." And in case the readers of their opinion would interpret it as praise for unmarried living, the court with poetic joy noted that "the joining of the man and woman in marriage is at once the most socially productive and individually fulfilling relationship that one can enjoy in the course of a lifetime."

One of the California Supreme Court Justices did disagree with the majority opinion. He believed that the court went farther than it had to in allowing Ms. Triola the relief she sought. This dissenter concluded in his last sentence, "By judicial overreach, the majority perform a . . . marriage, dissolve it, and distribute its property on terms never contemplated by the parties, case law, or the Legislature."

The bottom line of this case was that Lee Marvin was ordered to pay Michelle Triola Marvin $104,000. The court awarded Michelle Triola Marvin "$104,000 for rehabilitation purposes so that she may have the economic means to re-educate herself and to learn new, employable skills or to refurbish those utilized, for example, during her most recent employment and so that she may return from her status as companion of a motion picture star to a separate, independent but perhaps more prosaic existence." The court in a footnote observed that Ms. Triola "should be able to accomplish rehabilitation in less than two years. The sum awarded would be approximately equivalent to the highest scale that she ever earned as a singer, $1,000 per week, for two years."

In 1979 a New York court was called upon to look into a palimony situation involving rock star Peter Frampton.[21] This court held that Mrs. Penelope McCall, a woman who lived with Peter Frampton, could not recover damages for breach of an alleged oral contract in light of the fact that adultery was pleaded as the consideration—the price paid—for the alleged contract. Ms. McCall alleged that the condition of the contract she was to fulfill was leaving her husband, moving in with, and becoming associated with Frampton. The court held such an agreement void and unenforceable because it involved an illegality and was contrary to New York State's public policy, which favors matrimony.

In another case brought before a New York court one year earlier than the Frampton case, it was held that a woman who lived with a man for twenty-eight years, during which time he worked to support her and their three children, provided a home in their joint names, paid utility bills and taxes on the house, purchased the food and clothing for her and the children, and opened a joint bank account in their names, and further said that he would always "take care" of her, is entitled to temporary alimony upon dissolution of her nonmarital relationship on the ground of an implied contract.[22] This court found that the conduct of the woman constituted an implied promise not to work and to provide household services for her mate and their children in return for his promise to provide a home and future support. The court observed that the physical and mental anguish which may be visited upon a woman merely because of the lack of a ceremonial marriage requires that she be afforded protection in order to prevent "unjust enrichment" to the man.

The 1980s were ushered in with a New York decision which more clearly defined the palimony issue. New York's highest court held that an express contract between an unmarried couple would be enforceable.[23] However, this decision takes a stricter view of palimony than does California's Lee Marvin case because of its refusal to give validity to implied contracts between unmarried couples. As the court said, "We decline to follow the *Marvin* lead." The New York court observed that, "changing social custom has increased greatly the number of persons living together without solemnized ceremony." Despite this observation, New York is reluctant to give any legal basis for a palimony action unless there is an express contract between the two people.

WHERE ARE WE NOW?

Despite these various cases, which recognize certain property rights for unmarried couples, courts still have not awarded alimony in the case of a break-up between a man and woman who live together. The attitudes of society still permeate the law, namely, since the couple did not bother to get married, the courts shouldn't bother with their disputes; if the relationship was never made legally binding, then the couple is not entitled to legal remedies when things don't work out.

A recent Tennessee court decision best reflects how most courts still view the palimony issue.[24] The judge said that the "plaintiff and defendant lived together without the benefit of marriage and in this court's judgment, she 'committed inequity' and her action 'arises out of an immoral transaction.'" He added, "If these parties had been married, they would have been under the umbrella of legal protection." Reflecting the current moral standards of society, the court characterized such "live-in relationships" as "immoral" and "illegal." The judge declared, "He who has committed inequity shall not have equity and no right of action arises out of an immoral transaction." Throughout its decision, the court kept referring to "Pal-alimony." Apparently, the judge found it distasteful to even use the word palimony. Despite these stringent moral standards, even this judge could not totally ignore the woman's claim. He awarded her $3,000 because she entered the live-in relationship with a car and left without one. The judge was careful to make it clear that the $3,000 award was not based on equity or law but merely on an act of pity. He stated, "Lastly, plaintiff came on wheels and she left walking. The court feels that compassion—not justice or equity, but simple compassion—dictates that she have $3,000 to purchase a set of wheels for herself."

But as times change and more couples choose to live without the benefit of marriage, courts are going to be asked again and again to render justice regardless of the lack of a marriage ceremony. And while such a request might have been laughed out of court twenty and even ten years ago, the 1980s will see these requests increase—and that they are no laughing matter.

BERNIE AND PAT

Both Bernie and Pat had suffered bitter divorces. Each was gun-shy, and neither had any desire to tie the marital knot again. However, their occasional dates soon grew into a steady courtship, and eventually Bernie asked Pat to move in with him. The arrangement lasted for three years until Pat unexpectedly became pregnant. Bernie strongly urged abortion but because of her religious upbringing, Pat would not consider this option. She had the baby but not before Bernie moved out of the apartment. When Pat called him right after their baby was born, Bernie said he had no moral or legal obligation to support either Pat or their newborn son, Kevin. He pointed out it was her decision—not his—to have the child, and so she should bear the responsibility of raising him.

Bernie strongly held onto this position throughout the court proceedings that followed. Pat had no choice but to retain an attorney and seek support from Bernie because she was not able to support herself and her son without help. She did not want to get a job right away as she felt Kevin needed her total devotion for the first few years of life. Since Bernie earned more than $40,000 a year, she felt he should support her and Kevin, at least until it was time for her to leave Kevin and return to work. In all the proceedings that followed, Bernie never denied being the father. But he did argue that he was not responsible for supporting the child, since it was his decision that Pat should have an abortion, and therefore he was no longer responsible for the child. He contended that if he could not equally share in the decision whether or not to have the child, he should then not have the responsibility of supporting the child.

The court found it easy to reject Bernie's claim and ruled that Bernie's responsibility to support his child arose the second he was conceived. The court emphatically and unhesitatingly held that Bernie had to support Kevin until he reached adulthood.

However, it was much more difficult for the court to grapple with the issue of support for Pat. Pat urged the court to allow her alimony until Kevin entered kindergarten, so she would not have to go back to work during his important infant years. She argued that she should be treated no differently than a married woman, since Bernie and she had lived together as man and wife. She saw no reason why she and Kevin should be punished for lack of a marriage license. Bernie replied that there was no law which requires a man to pay alimony to his ex-girlfriend. The judge ruled in Bernie's favor and denied Pat alimony. She immediately appealed, and the case is still being considered by the Appellate Court.

The palimony issue still remains unresolved by most courts today. The lawmakers of the fifty states have been reluctant to delve into this touchy area. It's not a popular election issue either, so there will not be a rash of legislation passed to protect these relationships. If any rights are developed, they will most likely emerge from the judiciary through case law.

WHAT TO DO IF YOU AND YOUR FRIEND ARE PALS

It's obvious that the laws of most states are still unsettled when it comes to dealing with unmarried couples who break up. Court results depend more on the individual facts and equities of each particular case rather than on any broad and fixed principles of law.

If you live with someone in a state of unmatrimony, there is one legal fact that you can assume immediately. The courts will not be too sympathetic to your seeking any legal rights out of this nonlegal relationship. However, if you want to pin down some rights before potential trouble arises with your mate, you can draw a contract to spell out all of your economic obligations, duties, and rights to one another. Such a contract should be carefully made with legal assistance because it could be declared void by a court if it in any way relates to your sexual relationship, either directly or indirectly. If the agreement is drawn as a clear business one with terms of a purely economic nature, then there is a growing chance the courts will enforce it.

To further protect and clarify your rights, it would help to earmark any assets accumulated during the relationship as separate from your and your mate's personal property. For example, if you buy a house or make an investment, it would be wise to do so in joint name, as it will give each of you equal property rights in the asset regardless of your live-in relationship.

When it comes to children born out of wedlock, a couple can go to the local Family Court immediately upon the birth of the child and have a paternity order entered which once and forever gives the child a father. It's best to do this right away and while the unmarried father is sharing the joy of having a child and not two or three years later when the couple may be breaking up. Otherwise, there may be a fight not only for an equitable division of the assets but also over the question of who is the child's father. It's not unusual for an ex-boyfriend to deny paternity when the relationship goes sour. In other words, he can allege that his live-in girlfriend was having an illicit affair during the time of their illicit affair. This contention gives the man an extra bargaining edge which could be avoided by legally declaring him the father in Family Court at the time of birth.

Success in court always comes down to the hard facts and the evidence presented. This rule applies in a courtroom battle over palimony. If a woman wants to establish that she is entitled to some economic "benefit" out of an illicit relationship, she will have to prove quite convincingly to a court that principles of fairness and equity demand that she receive a financial award. To do this, she must produce clear facts that sustain her position. She must be able to produce financial books, accounts, records, data, documents, and witnesses, all of which prove that she put a lot more into the relationship than her body, companionship, social talent, and homemaking skills. If she can prove that she gave or produced economic benefit to her mate, or sacrificed economic benefits of her own, then a court of equity might make him share with her or at least reimburse her for the value he received.

It should be mentioned here that there is, of course, one sure way for a happily unmarried couple seeking legal protection for their relationship—marriage!

Chapter 5
GAYLIMONY

The Gay Rights Movement has brought yet another area of the alimony controversy more and more to the fore. The everyday problems of homosexuals have not been a concern to the general community because such lifestyles were kept private. Homoscxuals rarely turned to the general community to solve personal problems because of society's intolerant attitude. And they didn't turn to the law for help because they didn't think the courts would be sympathetic to their problems—a reasonably correct assessment.

As gay life is now more open, there is less reluctance on the part of a homosexual to seek help from the legal community and from the courts. And as might be expected, many of these personal problems involve other homosexuals. Battles between gays who are breaking up, while usually free of such divisive issues as custody, child support and visitation, are often bitterly fought over the division of property accumulated during their "married" life. It is increasingly common for a lawyer to be asked to draw a "property settlement" agreement between battling gay mates, and such contracts are as binding upon each as any contract is between any two people. It is even more common for a gay couple to enter into a written "pre-marriage" contract which defines their rights and obligations and provides for division of property in the event of a parting of the ways.

A recent California case enforced just such an agreement between lesbians.[25] In 1978 a Superior Court Judge ordered a lesbian spouse to pay her "wife" $100 per month in temporary support. The judge based his decision on contract theory and not on marital duty to support. This couple had executed a written pre-marriage agreement one week before their church ceremony. Their contract specifically provided that the couple would divide any property accumulated during their relationship in the event they separated. The agreement also included a term which provided that the "wife" was not to work during the relationship, while the "husband" was to work and be the provider. The judge ordered gaylimony by holding the agreement binding on the parties.

A court of law may enforce such contractual agreements as it would enforce any contract between two people. But the court may be required to throw the agreement out the window if it in any way relates to the illicit sexual relationship between the parties on the ground that it violates public policy. Likewise, in ending a relationship, parting homosexuals will have to mutually agree to a "property settlement" agreement because courts are not yet prone to impose any rights or obligations on the relationship, apart from the gays' own agreement. Once again, while a court might enforce an agreement, it is unlikely to order a "divorce" or "separation." So far, courts at most will take a passive role in settling disputes between homosexuals.

The concept that the homosexual in America has

the same rights to life, liberty, and the pursuit of happiness as does the heterosexual is one that is slowly emerging. In time, society may recognize homosexual relationships. If a man and woman live together and share an economic, social, and personal life interwoven with rights, duties, and obligations, and if equity demands a restoration of economic balance between them when their relationship ends, then such an award will also be justified between two men or two women living together. In other words, the gender of the mates may someday make no difference under the law.

In Washington, D. C., a $100,000 gaylimony suit was filed in 1979 by a man against his male spouse for his failing to live up to a verbal agreement, to "support, provide him with board, maintenance, clothing, medical expenses and other necessities, and share half the profits of a real estate venture."[26] The attorneys for both sides of this dispute admit that their litigation was spurred by the Lee Marvin palimony decision.

BARRY AND AL

When they first met at the home of a friend, Barry and Al were unaware of each other's sexual preference. They just seemed to hit it off and over the next month they spent increasing time together playing tennis or going to the movies. Barry was a buyer at a leading department store and Al was a real estate broker. In time, they discovered to their mutual joy that each was gay. Before long, they had set up house together. They neither flaunted nor were ashamed of their love, and their families and friends accepted their relationship for what it was—two people sharing their lives. They led their lives together privately and without fanfare. While sympathetic to the Gay Rights Movement, they did not march in parades, and their fellow workers were unaware of their homosexual "marriage." Barry and Al reasoned that their lifestyle was no one else's business.

They lived in an atmosphere of contentment for eight years. They purchased beachfront property on a nearby island. They bought a condominium in the city in their joint names. They furnished both properties nicely. Barry and Al considered themselves a married couple, and sharing was an important part of their marriage. Whenever they bought property or stock, or put money in the bank, it was in both names.

Trouble arose in their ninth year of "marriage." Barry and Al had always spent a great deal of time with Al's college roommate, Gordon. Gordon and his wife, Mary, and their two young children spent weekends at the beach and dropped in at Barry and Al's home without even the formality of a phone call. They were like one big happy family, and in fact Gordon and Mary's children called Barry and Al "uncle." Because of this closeness, Barry and Al were deeply distressed when they discovered their best friends were having marital problems. And as is often the case when people have problems, Gordon turned to a friend—Barry—for help. Gordon met Barry frequently for lunch or for long evening walks to discuss his problems with Mary. Al encouraged Barry to give his ex-roommate all the help and time he needed. Al viewed Mary as the perfect wife for Gordon and hoped Barry would find the key to Gordon's discontent. Much to

Barry's initial shock, he did—Gordon was in love with Barry! The discovery was a mixed one for Barry. Over the years, he had grown strongly attached to Gordon but never imagined Gordon would have feelings for him—at least not sexual. Even more important, Barry still loved Al and now felt torn between the security and stability of Al's love and the unexpected and exciting prospect of life with Gordon. As soon as Gordon revealed his innermost feelings to Barry, he found it imperative to end his marriage no matter what decision Barry came to. Gordon filed for a divorce and moved into an apartment. By then, Barry had told Al what had happened, leaving Al bewildered. Soon after, Barry moved in with Gordon, and Al went to see his lawyer.

It was only then that Al found he and Barry had been living unrealistically. During their nine happy years together, the Gay Rights Movement never seemed to relate directly to them. Secure jobs, good friends, and mutual contentment insulated them from community prejudice. Al's lawyer told him the facts of life. His relationship with Barry was immoral and illegal in the eyes of the law and of the community at large. Barry could walk out on him anytime he wanted to, and there was nothing Al could do about it—legally or otherwise. Nor could Al run to court for support, alimony, or a "divorce." Mary could name Barry as a co-respondent in her divorce action against Gordon, but Al had no legal forum to complain. They may have considered themselves married, but this was simply not so. When Al pointed out to his lawyer that Barry was his main support because he had assumed the household chores during the past nine years and had let his real estate efforts slack off, he was informed that the law would not do a thing about that.

But the lawyer did prepare an agreement that helped Al and Barry divide the property accumulated during their "marriage." He even succeeded in including a provision to give Al $200 a week "gaylimony" for two years. Barry agreed to the provision, even though he was advised there was no way Al would get this support in court. He signed the agreement for two reasons. First, Barry recognized that Al did in fact devote most of his time to caring for the household while letting his business languish. Second, Barry still cared for Al and carried a great deal of guilt over what had happened. He felt responsible for Gordon's leaving Mary, for his leaving Al, and for the bitter end of Al's longtime friendship with Gordon. In short, Barry was willing to pay both to ease his conscience and to deal fairly with Al.

For the first few months after the signing of the agreement, Al went off the deep end. He quickly accepted Barry's weekly checks, but refused to have anything to do with Gordon or Barry. He spent most of his time barhopping and with one-night stands. With each brief encounter, Al's personality took a turn for the worse, and Barry's understanding withered away. Barry's attitude changed from sorrow, to pity, to anger. It was then that Barry cut off the weekly "gaylimony" payments. Al ran to his lawyer. Legal action was started to enforce the terms of their contract, but it was quickly dismissed by an unsympathetic judge.

The court reasoned that while certain

agreements could be binding between homosexuals, the one between Barry and Al was primarily based upon their immoral relationship and so was unenforceable. The judge held it would be against the state's public policy and the community's morals to allow homosexuals to have legal rights arising from their sexual relationship. Al's lawyer had argued eloquently that the agreement was based solely on economic considerations, but the judge did not buy the argument. He simply noted that Al's need for Barry's support was directly related to their sexual relationship, which resulted in Al's withdrawal from the work force and his economic dependency on Barry.

TRANSALIMONY

One way for a man to avoid alimony, albeit a mind-boggling one, is to become a woman. If courts are thrown by palimony and gaylimony, imagine their distress with cases involving transsexuals!

A transsexual is an individual who is predisposed to identify with the opposite sex. It is estimated that 2,000 to 3,000 persons have undergone sex change operations in the United States during the past ten years. The anomaly of a transsexual's identification often throws the law into a quandary. A 1970 English case involved the validity of a marriage of a post-operative transsexual and a man.[27] In that case, the English judge held that the transsexual had failed to prove that she had changed her sex from male to female, and, therefore, their marriage was void on the ground that it could never be consummated. Basically, that court held that an individual's sex is fixed at birth, can never be changed, and marriage is heterosexual in character.

However, the most recent American case disagreed with this English case and specifically noted that the reasoning of the judge was incorrect. A New Jersey court held in 1976 that a husband had a legal obligation to pay alimony to his wife despite the fact that the wife had been a male.[28] In this case, the plaintiff underwent an operation in 1971 for removal of male sex organs and construction of a vagina. In fact, the prospective husband paid for the surgery. Approximately a year after this sex reassignment operation, the two were married in New York State and then moved back to New Jersey. They consummated the marriage, although, of course, no children were born. Two years later, the husband abandoned his wife and failed to support her. She then went to the New Jersey court and filed for alimony. The husband argued that she was a male and that the marriage was therefore void. The court rejected the defense and held that the wife was, at the time of her marriage, female and that the defendant, who was a man, became her lawful husband and was obligated to support her. The court ruled that a true transsexual who surgically changes her external sexual anatomy from male to female truly becomes a member of the opposite sex. The court reasoned that such a transsexual has the capacity to enter a marriage and live as "man and wife" with a member of the opposite sex, formerly a member of her own sex—physically speaking, that is.

Other courts have come to contrary conclusions. The New Jersey case does not fall in line with several New York cases dealing with the rights of transsexuals. In one New York case, the court held such a marriage void. In that case, the two mates never had sexual intercourse and in fact had not lived together.[29] It was claimed that the defendant was a transsexual who had surgery to remove his male organs after the marriage. In another New York case, a female transsexual had had a hysterectomy and mastectomy but had not received any male organs and was incapable of performing sexually as a male.[30] He then married a female, who later sued for annulment on the ground that he had defrauded her by not informing her of his transsexuality and of the operation. The New York court in that case held that even if the defendant was a male trapped in the body of a female, his attempted sex-reassignment surgery had not successfully released him from that body.

Chapter 6
PREMARITAL CONTRACTS: THE DEATH OF ROMANCE?

Matt and Nancy met during their senior year of college, fell desperately in love, and within weeks were talking about marriage. Their discussions differed greatly from those of their parents who took each other home for parent approval, and from their grandparents who had the decision made for them by their parents. Matt and Nancy consulted their attorneys and asked them to draw up an ironclad premarital contract which protected each of them in the event of a possible divorce.

Times have changed! Now many couples have extensive negotiations prior to marriage. We've come a long way since the '60s and '70s when the concept of "trying on the shoe" was prevalent. The 1980s and '90s may be less concerned over shoe size and more concerned about guarantees, rebates, trade-ins, and latent defects.

Carrying the premarriage contract to its logical extreme, we end up with an automatic termination of a marriage with an option to renew. This term-marriage concept is being seriously explored by several states. The Alaskan Legislature in 1980 considered a bill giving the stamp of legality to disposable marriages. The proposed legislation would allow a couple to get married for a term of five years, at the end of which the marriage would be automatically dissolved, although it could be renewed upon mutual consent. The proponents of such intriguing marital concepts contend that such "disposable" marriages would reduce the divorce rate and the bitter squabbling that goes along with a marriage breakup. While an interesting idea, no state has yet enacted such short-term marriage contracts, nor do these kinds of renewable marriages seem to have sufficient legislative support to take hold in the near future.

But the incidence of premarriage contracts—what the law calls antenuptial agreements—is increasing. They are hardly romantic documents. Frequently, they are drawn up when the groom wants to limit the amount of money his bride will receive upon divorce or at his death. The law recognizes these agreements and gives them the same binding effect as any other contract.

The classic antenuptial agreement is between a wealthy older man and his fourth wife-to-be, a young twenty-eight year old. At eighty-two, his life expectancy is short, and often his primary concern is that this young lady is marrying him for love and not for his money. To reassure himself, he asks her to sign an agreement prepared by his lawyers, which waives her rights to his estate in exchange for a certain limited sum of money she will receive upon his death. Because he holds the deck of cards, the young (and perhaps shrewd) woman usually signs the agreement. She doesn't want to ruin her prospects for this marriage. And why shouldn't she sign an agreement giving her $250,000 upon his death? At this point, his net worth of $15,000,000 is beyond her reach anyway. They marry, and he dies three years later. She then immediately hires a lawyer to challenge the agreement. The typical claims are that she did not read the agreement before she signed it, didn't understand its meaning, didn't have an attorney, couldn't read English, had a limited education, didn't know the true nature of her husband's worth and finally, that he deceived her into signing the paper and was guilty of fraud.

If this typical case is pursued all the way through the courts, the odds are that the young widow will lose. These contracts are binding and are usually drawn in such a way as to be ironclad. But what usually happens is that the case is settled long before it ever reaches court and the estate pays off the "grieving" widow. Since these estates are usually substantial, the last thing the rest of the family wants is a bitter court fight which will tie up all of their money until the claim is finally settled. Rather than be unable to use the full estate assets for many years, the estate often prefers to give some additional money to the surviving spouse. So if the young widow's share would be one-third of the estate ($5,000,000 in the case above), assuming she had the agreement invalidated, the estate may make a compromise offer of one million to end the conflict.

Perhaps the most well publicized premarital agreement in recent memory was between Jacqueline Bouvier Kennedy and her second husband, Aristotle Onassis. While not the typical couple, their situation still illustrates the advantages and pitfalls of premarital planning. While the terms were not revealed, it is known that the two entered an extensive and intricate premarital agreement just before their marriage, and that the terms were created with great care and concern. The agreement purportedly covered all aspects of their relationship, including provisions in the event of a marriage break-up, the death of either party, and care for their children. According to Stephen Birmingham in his book titled *Jacqueline Bouvier Kennedy Onassis*:

Among other things, Onassis agreed to give Jackie $3,000,000 in tax-free bonds outright. Further, she was not required to give Onassis a child. The pair agreed that they only needed to spend Catholic and summer holidays together and that, for the rest of the time, they could come and go and live as they wished, and where they wished. They agreed that separate bedrooms would be provided for each whenever both were under the same roof. If the couple decided to separate, the following provisions were strictly set up: If Ari left Jackie, he would give her $10,000,000 for each year of the marriage; if Jackie left Ari within five years, she would receive only $20,000,000; if she left him after five years, she would receive $20,000,000 plus a trust fund of $180,000 for the next ten years. If Ari died while still married to Jackie, she would get $100,000,000. If Jackie died before her husband, all her property and money would go to her children, but they would be supported by Onassis until each was twenty-one years old.

Despite the battery of lawyers employed to insure an airtight agreement which would successfully repel any future attack, it still failed to prevent legal action after the death of Mr. Onassis. A subsequent settlement was reached between Mrs. Onassis and the estate of her late husband which purportedly differed from the terms of the premarital agreement; she received more than the amount agreed upon.

As is evident, while a premarital agreement can attempt to spell out the rights and obligations of the couple before their marriage, it can never guarantee freedom from litigation in the future. On the other hand, if

57

well-thought out and carefully drawn, a premarital contract can at least create a broad framework for a settlement at the time of separation, divorce, or death and at most, be binding on the couple when their relationship ends.

A more common use of antenuptial agreements is where two senior citizens, each widowed, decide to share their remaining years together as companions, friends, and lovers. Veterans of long, happy marriages to their first spouses, neither really expects the same depth from the new marital relationship. Most important, neither wants a new mate to inherit his or her estate. Both have grown children and grandchildren to whom they want to leave their assets. To assure this, they can enter into an antenuptial agreement in which each waives rights to the other's estate.

Premarital agreements can also be used to spell out or limit the amount of alimony to be paid in the event the prospective marriage fails. For example, if an eighty-two-year-old tycoon is afraid his young love merely intends to live with him a short while to earn the right to receive alimony, he can have her stipulate in their antenuptial agreement the amount of alimony she will receive in the event a divorce occurs.

A word of caution: the most careful premarital negotiations and the ultimate signing of a detailed premarital contract are not intended to assure a long and happy marriage as much as they are meant to assure an easy and quick end to the marriage. Critics contend these premarital steps encourage a quick dropout from marriage as soon as any degree of satisfaction wanes.

ELINOR AND ROY

After two divorces, Roy was skittish about his impending marriage to Elinor. For her, it was a simple matter of absolute, unqualified love in the most romantic sense; for Roy it was just one more attempt at making marriage work. What scared Roy most was not the risk of failure but the potentially bitter divorce battle if his third try did not work. So it made sense to Roy to draw up a premarital contract which would stipulate the terms of a potential divorce. Roy broached the idea gingerly with Elinor but his fears proved groundless; Elinor would have done anything Roy asked. Elinor didn't really read the document in Roy's lawyer's office because it seemed so academic to her. Her marriage to Roy was going to be forever, and she was most sympathetic to his fears of the marital institution. She knew Roy's first two wives did not understand him and did not have the great capacity to love him as she did.

After three years of marriage, Elinor's feelings had not changed, but Roy had begun to tire of his third wife. He spent his evenings prowling around town, and when he did return home, he continually abused his starry-eyed wife. What turned him off most of all was her slavish devotion to him, which seemed to increase with his abuse of her. Finally, Roy could no longer stand the sight of Elinor, and he filed for divorce.

Elinor felt as if she had been struck by lightning. For days she was in shock and could not accept the fact that Roy wanted to end what she considered a "perfect" marriage. She dragged herself to her parents' home, and they gave her support, consolation, and a topflight attorney. Her lawyer immediately filed for alimony and counsel fees, and that's when he first learned about the premarital agreement. When he confronted Elinor with the contract, she could not even remember signing it. She had forgotten the document Roy had asked her to sign as his insurance against divorce. When she signed, she did not even know what alimony was, and now she discovered she had waived her right to receive it.

Her lawyer attempted to invalidate the contract by arguing that Elinor had not read it carefully and signed it only to please Roy. The judge held the agreement to be binding on her and said that while Elinor's love was blind, it was still no defense for her failure to read a contract she signed.

But despite increasing interest in premarital contracts, most couples do not view their forthcoming marriage in such a cold and calculating manner. Romance has not been dispensed with, by any means. Regardless of age, ethnic group, economic or educational background, the typical couple who stands before a clergyman or judge does so with solemnity, deep feeling, and hope for a beautiful future together. In years past, a judge would always read the traditional legal marriage formula spelled out in the lawbooks; legal, but dry and unromantic. Now, many couples ask the judge to read their own marriage ceremony or ask him to create a more personal and meaningful one for them.

Few couples take their vows with alimony on their minds. Yet, no matter how one approaches marriage, the continually escalating divorce rate is not likely to slow up in the 1980s. A mechanism which can ease the trauma of a divorce should be encouraged and used when possible; hence, the validity of premarital contracts.

Chapter 7
SEPARATION: THE END OR A NEW BEGINNING?

Psychological preparedness is the key to successful divorce and life thereafter. You may have a thousand good reasons to get rid of your mate, but unless you're psychologically prepared to face a new life for yourself, it may be the wrong time to shed your partner. In almost every divorce, at least one spouse is afraid of the future, usually the one who doesn't want the divorce. As bad as a marriage may be, many people would rather live within the security of an unhappy status quo than risk going from the frying pan into the fire. Many tolerate poor, if not downright horrid, marriages because they're afraid of venturing into the unknown.

The most bitterly fought divorces are caused not by dispute over support, custody or visitation rights, but because of fear of the unknown which at the last minute provides the mental block to a final termination of the marriage. The most typical symptom of this kind of divorce battle is the "one more thing" syndrome. Negotiations seem endless, and just when every little issue appears to have been hammered out, something new pops up to block final settlement. The party not ready for the divorce will invariably find one more problem to raise.

Even mutual decisions to divorce do not occur overnight. They often evolve over months or years of agonized doubt until the mates decide living apart will be better than living together. The reasons behind the ultimate conclusion are as varied as each individual.

Divorce is such a final and devastating concept that many couples grasp first for separation as a way station. Whether used as a method to adjust to the trauma of final termination or as an attempt to save a faltering relationship, separation usually does no more than postpone the inevitable.

The beauty of a separation agreement is that it provides a framework for provisions which suit the parties and meet their own particular needs. It's a most effective tool for negotiating a mutually satisfactory resolution to marital differences. And there's no limit to the creative approaches that can be taken. For example, it's generally accepted that alimony should cease when the wife remarries. But in drafting separation agreements, the attorney for the husband is often concerned about the scope of such a remarriage provision. If the agreement provides, "Said wife is to receive a hundred dollars a week alimony for as long as she lives or until she remarries," she might be discouraged from seeking a new mate for sound economic reasons, e.g., she doesn't want to lose her weekly payments. To get around this problem, there are innovative approaches which can encourage her remarriage. The agreement can state that, "Said wife shall receive a hundred dollars a week alimony for as long as she lives or until she remarries and that upon said remarriage, said wife shall receive a lump sum payment of $12,500." Such a provision serves several purposes. It provides for the wife's care. It gives her a generous wedding present from her ex-husband if she decides to

62

try marriage again. She is less reluctant to get serious about another man. It also gives the ex-husband hope that he might one day be released from such financial obligations. Finally, it's a novel way for the wife to have a dowry.

Whatever terms are finally decided upon, a separation agreement encompasses much more than an agreement to separate. It is the written contract which includes all of the conditions for final termination of the marriage. It might be more appropriately called a divorce agreement.

The purpose of such an agreement is obvious: it attempts to settle all issues between the disputing marriage partners and defines all of their rights, duties, and obligations to one another and to their children. Like any contract, it has a binding effect on the parties. Without such a written agreement, spouses can spend years going in and out of court to fight over each issue, however small. A good separation agreement resolves all of the differences once and for all and ties them together in one neat comprehensive package. The next step is the divorce itself.

Chapter 8
CHOOSING A LAWYER

The most important decision you will have to make in getting a divorce is choosing the right lawyer. It may make the difference between a quick, easy divorce and a drawn out, bitter one; it may make the difference between a good economic settlement and one that leaves you in impossible financial straits, perhaps for the rest of your life. But the selection of a lawyer is usually the one aspect of a divorce which gets the least care and attention from battling spouses. If you make a random choice, you'll have opted for playing Russian roulette with your life—but the odds aren't nearly as good.

How do you pick the right lawyer? Begin by asking members of your family and friends. If you know a particular lawyer, perhaps with whom you've dealt in the past (your will, buying a house) and in whom you have faith, consider that person first. However, the best real estate lawyer or finest estate attorney may be the worst matrimonial lawyer. The frightening fact is that they may take your case if you ask them. Most cities have legal reference services, and you can call your local Bar Association for this information. Still, a legal reference service will only give you the names of a few attorneys, without a candid discussion of their ability. The bottom line, therefore, is your initial interview with a lawyer.

When you have found a lawyer, make an appointment to discuss your marital situation. Most lawyers do not charge for an initial interview, although this is something you can check when you call for an appointment. Such an interview usually lasts for half an hour to an hour. You will probably do most of the talking at first. Discuss your situation openly. The lawyer will then tell you in broad terms what he or she can do for you. Ask how he plans to achieve the goals you seek. Just as it is your goal to evaluate him as an attorney, it is his to evaluate you as a client and learn how he can achieve your objectives. At this point, you should be able to tell if his attitude is right for your case. However, despite your exchange with the lawyer, there is no reason for you to make a snap judgment. Rather than hiring on the spot, it is usually best to mull it over for a bit. Before leaving, you should ask what the overall fee will be for the legal services. While the price of your divorce must necessarily depend on the work to be done in the future, most lawyers will quote you a fee, barring unforeseen circumstances which might complicate your case.

It is important that you find a lawyer in whom you have faith and with whom you feel comfortable. If these essentials are missing, the best lawyer in the world will still not be the right one for you. Confidence in your lawyer, your ease in communicating, and your belief that he or she truly knows you and what you want out of your case are the kinds of gut feelings you must not ignore.

If upon reflection, you like the lawyer and feel that the advice is sound and that you will be well served, hire that person. If you are in doubt, tell him you want to think it over. Make an appointment with another lawyer.

Repeat this process until you find the lawyer you want. Only you can judge whether a lawyer is right for you. Your instinct, common sense, and rapport with the lawyer should lead you to the right choice.

The vital point to remember is that your lawyer is working for you. If you are not happy with him, you have the right to discharge him and seek other counsel. It is far worse to remain with a lawyer in whom you have lost confidence. You will only question everything he does which will undermine any effectiveness he has in representing you. You should not be deterred by concern about his feelings or his fee, or what a new lawyer is going to think; by firing a lawyer you're unhappy with you'll be doing both your lawyer and yourself a favor.

If you do choose to fire your lawyer, don't rush out and hire the next lawyer you find. Instead, repeat the process of careful selection.

PEACEMAKER vs. KILLER

Depending on the kind of case you have, you may want a tough lawyer to battle for you without giving an inch and without compromise. Or, you may find your particular case more suited for a gentleman lawyer who, by his nature, is likely to work things out amicably. If your spouse is reasonable and generally concurs with you, the best approach would be to hire a lawyer who has the ability to work out a compatible divorce. On the other hand, if you are attempting to shed a difficult mate, or if you are trying to prevent your spouse from shedding you, then you'll want to hire a tough lawyer. In these latter situations, common sense tells you that there will be no easy way to resolve your case, so you might as well be prepared for the worst: get the best protection for yourself where you'll need it the most—in the courtroom.

BIG FIRM vs. SOLE PRACTITIONER

Another choice you may have to make is whether to hire a lawyer from a big firm or a sole practitioner. As litigation gets more complex, more and more lawyers are forming firms or joining large established firms, rather than going it alone. Not even the best lawyer can be in two courts at once, and there are a lot of advantages to a firm with several lawyers who cover for each other and share the work load. To the client, there are both advantages and disadvantages.

With a large firm, you always know there will be someone there to handle your case and answer your questions. Even though only one lawyer will be assigned to your case, other associates in the firm may be familiar with the case, or at least may be able to answer your questions and handle any emergencies that arise if your primary lawyer is not available.

With a one-man office, your lawyer may be much harder to locate and communicate with. If he gets sick or takes a vacation, you have nowhere to turn. On the other hand, the advantage of the single practitioner is that he and he alone is responsible for your case. Your case is his personal concern; it isn't assigned or delegated to anyone else. This personal treatment may be missing in a larger firm which handles vast amounts of litigation, keeps exact timesheets, and has all levels of lawyers taking care of various aspects of your case depending on their importance, ranging from the senior partner who receives $200 an hour through the junior partner at $125 an hour, to the senior associate at $85 an hour down to the bottom rung of the law firm ladder, the new lawyer fresh out of law school who charges the "humiliating" sum of only $75 an hour. Matrimonial matters are by their very nature extremely personal, and larger firms may appear too impersonal to a distraught spouse seeking solace, warmth, and understanding.

These observations are, of course, generalizations; the fact remains that the most important criteria is not whether your lawyer has a little cubbyhole where he practices alone or shares a large suite of offices with other lawyers, as much as whether you like him and whether you feel he is competent.

COMPETENT vs. INCOMPETENT

It would seem obvious that you would want a competent lawyer. Believe it or not, sometimes there can be a peculiar advantage to having an extremely incompetent lawyer. If your spouse wants out of the marriage, but you want to hold on or at least do everything you can to block his path to freedom, it may be to your advantage to have the most bumbling attorney around; you'll certainly be throwing a monkey wrench in your mate's plan to end the marriage. This strategy is called "checkmate." Many a marital contest has been thrown off the track because of the lawyers and not the clients. It is not unusual to hear a lawyer bemoan an impossible case because of his adversary's incompetence. A bad lawyer will make the wrong motion, neglect to properly file papers, move for permission to correct his mistake, make the wrong demands in negotiations, misinterpret his own client's wishes, or fail to understand the favorable offers of his adversary to end the marriage, with the result that the other lawyer becomes exasperated and the case helplessly stuck in a quagmire of legal mistakes. However, rather than purposely retaining an incompetent lawyer, it is far better in the long run to have a competent one who can take steps to stall your case. For most clients, the problem is not choosing between a competent or an incompetent attorney, but distinguishing between the two. Unfortunately, it's not unusual to accidentally hire an incompetent attorney in your search for a competent one. Then you are in trouble!

MATRIMONIAL EXPERT vs. GENERAL PRACTITIONER

The minute you have a marriage problem, many of your friends and family members will tell you to see so and so, reputed to be the matrimonial or divorce lawyer in your town. There is a lot to be said for hiring an expert in any field, but there's also no question that a good general practitioner is always better than a lousy specialist. However, the *competent* specialist's greater familiarity with his field should give him the necessary edge.

Yet, one still has to exercise caution in picking a matrimonial expert. He may have particular prejudices or limitations which impair his ability to represent you well. For example, some divorce specialists are known to favor the husband's or the wife's side. Another potential problem with a marital expert is that he might unnecessarily complicate a rather simple divorce because of his extensive knowledge of the field. By and large, however, a divorce lawyer has that extra know-how to do a better job for you.

YOUTH vs. AGE

An outstanding reputation and distinguished credentials established over a long career are impressive and are often what make an older lawyer initially more appealing than a younger one. You may even feel honored that such a lawyer would have the time to take your little case. But does this mean he will do a good job for you?

At the other extreme is your next door neighbor's niece who got her law degree last June. At 24, she is full of vim, vigor, and knowledge of the law. However, she has no clients. The two things she can offer you are plenty of time on your case and a low price for your divorce. But will she do a good job for you in your divorce battle?

Your criterion for hiring a lawyer should not be based on age. Youth versus experience has been analyzed in every profession; the law is no exception. In the final analysis, it is the lawyer and his or her ability to serve you well which matters.

A brief caveat: Be careful about basing your choice on reputation. Many lawyers have established fine reputations, but at some point many have also begun to ride on those reputations.

SHOULD YOU HIRE A WOMAN LAWYER?

The legal system may still be dominated by chauvinistic thinking, but even that is bound to change as more and more women enter this once almost exclusively male domain. Only a decade or two ago, most law schools had very few women in each class. Now the enrollment in most law schools is one-third female. With so many women entering the profession, clients now have the option of selecting a woman attorney to handle their case. Furthermore, the odds are increasing that your case may be decided by a woman jurist.

Should it matter to you whether your divorce lawyer is male or female? Maybe. Assuming that difference in gender makes no difference in competence, there might be psychological advantages in having a woman lawyer. Many wives are so fed up with their husbands that they have little faith in any man. They would much rather be represented by a woman lawyer and would have greater faith—the element vital to a successful attorney-client relationship—in a woman lawyer.

On the other hand, don't expect a woman lawyer to automatically sympathize with a woman's plight. Women attorneys have to fight continually as minority members of their profession, and they may believe that a wife should be able to stand on her own two feet and fight for what's rightfully hers. They've worked hard to be where they are and expect other women to be able to do the same. Because of this attitude, many divorcing husbands choose a competent woman attorney to represent them. When the husband's female lawyer argues that the wife should go out and get a job, she may appear more credible than the male attorney who says the same thing.

One additional factor should be noted, and that's the attitude of the male members of the legal profession toward female members. Many male attorneys do not appreciate this invasion of their ranks and still hold a degree of disdain for the woman lawyer. One particular gripe of many male attorneys is that a woman attorney always has a "chip on her shoulder" and "is out to prove something." Because of this attitude, the male attorney sometimes assumes that any case in which he has to deal with a woman lawyer will be extremely difficult to work out. He would much rather negotiate with another man. Of course, this may increase the chances that a woman lawyer will behave as though she has a "chip on her legal shoulder," and this may be to the advantage or disadvantage of her client depending on the circumstances. In any case, it's a factor that can't be ignored.

ESTABLISHMENT LAWYER vs. MAVERICK

When you are searching for an attorney, people will often tell you to hire a particular one because he's been around and knows all the judges well. Someone linked to the legal or judicial establishment will supposedly achieve a better result for you. On the other hand, you may be told to avoid a certain lawyer because he breaks all the rules and has, at one time or another, aroused the animosity of other lawyers and judges.

Whether you hire a maverick or an accepted establishment lawyer, your case is still going to rise or fall on whether he's a good lawyer and whether he spends the time necessary to get results for you. Even the most outstanding lawyer is no good to you if he doesn't spend time on your case.

There might be an advantage in hiring a maverick if you have the kind of case which is unpopular or which seeks to break new ground in the law. For instance, a lawyer with individuality and flair might be able to convince a judge to award palimony to a girlfriend deserted by her boyfriend or, in a novel case, where a husband is seeking alimony. Other than that, your main concern should not be that your lawyer is a maverick or a legal bore, but whether or not he works hard on your case and does his best to get results for you.

A LOCAL ATTORNEY vs. AN OUT-OF-TOWN "NAME"

You might feel there is no local attorney good enough to handle your case, and so you are attracted to a "name" matrimonial lawyer from outside your community. Whether he's from the next town or the big city down the river, there can be disadvantages to hiring an out-of-town attorney, no matter how good he is.

The main problem is communicating with him. One of the more important considerations in choosing a lawyer is his proximity, so that you can easily reach him to discuss your problems. In marital disputes, problems arise on a daily or at least a weekly basis. Therefore, you must have quick and easy access to your lawyer. The second problem with an out-of-town lawyer is his lack of familiarity with local legal practices in your community. There's always an advantage to being in home territory, and the out-of-town lawyer is therefore at a loss in this regard.

Generally speaking, retaining an attorney from a different town or city puts the client at a disadvantage, and it should only be resorted to if you live in that rare community that lacks at least a few good lawyers.

DO-IT-YOURSELF DIVORCE: THE FOOL'S WAY

After considering the various possibilities, you might conclude that it's best not to hire a lawyer. This alternative is not as farfetched as it once was because there has been a definite trend toward "Do-It-Yourself" law and, in particular, "Do-It-Yourself Divorces." Individuals and companies sell do-it-yourself divorce kits at a minimal cost which purport to guide you to divorce court at a substantial saving over hiring an attorney. Not only do you save a tremendous amount of money by doing it yourself, the ad copy claims, but you also avoid the possibility of hiring one of those lawyers whose main ability is to botch up cases.

There are people, of course, who can do almost anything themselves. We all know someone who is a do-it-yourself plumber, mechanic, lawyer, dentist, and nuclear scientist all rolled into one. Ending a marriage, however, requires more than the ability to repair a refrigerator. There are divorces which are rather simple, but the difficulty lies in being able to predict in advance which divorce is simple and which is going to suddenly turn complicated and ugly.

What often appears to be the easiest case turns out to be the most bitter and complex one. By the same token, it is not unusual for the apparent hard case to settle quite quickly. Rather than chance compounding your problems by not knowing what you're doing, hire a good lawyer. Even when you and your mate appear to agree totally on all of the terms of your divorce, you may both be overlooking a significant matter which, if ignored, will cost you dearly after the divorce. If you fail to tie all loose ends together, don't take advantage of all tax considerations, neglect to spell out in detail all of the terms of the divorce, or inadvertently make some terms of your divorce ambiguous or leave them out altogether, you invite trouble later on. The old adage still serves: "Anyone who handles his own case has a fool for a client."

HOW TO BE A GOOD CLIENT

This is an aspect of a lawyer-client relationship that is

rarely addressed. A "bad" client can seriously hamper the success of his or her lawyer. To use an analogy, you may have the finest dentist in the world, but if you suddenly move after he tells you to remain perfectly still, he might inadvertently do some damage in your mouth. Cooperation between a client and attorney is vital.

What characterizes a good client? Honesty is first and foremost. Many clients feel if they conceal facts which are damaging to their case, their lawyer will be better able to defend them. For instance, the husband fighting alimony might not tell his lawyer that he has a weekend job which gives him an additional one-hundred-dollars-a-week income because he wants his lawyer to go to court believing that he has only his five-day-a-week job which earns him $250 a week. He hopes his lawyer will argue with great eloquence and convince the judge that he can't pay much alimony on $250 a week. It's pretty obvious what the judge is going to do when the wife's lawyer walks in with surprise witnesses and proves that the husband is hiding his weekend job. But it's the husband's own attorney who is furious. Not because he looks foolish in his ignorance, but more important, because he could have prevented the courtroom surprise.

As a client you should immediately tell your lawyer anything significant that has happened or is happening in your marriage. You need not mention trivia which may cause him to turn a deaf ear to your valid remarks. Keep in mind that your lawyer is there to serve you, and you should feel comfortable to call him whenever necessary. Be sure to immediately convey to him any information you might think useful for your case. For example: You discover the name of your spouse's new "friend"; you discover that your spouse is making extra money on the side; you find that your children are being neglected or, worse, abused; you learn that your wife went on an unbelievable shopping spree; you hear that your husband is about to clean out your joint account;

you learn that your spouse is seeking medical attention and may have cancer. The list is, of course, endless. Factors that are important are those that could substantially affect the outcome of your case. If there's any doubt, call your lawyer.

Another rule which is vital to good attorney-client relations is the payment of the fee. No one likes to pay a lawyer—especially someone who feels he's the innocent party. But a busy lawyer has many clients and limited time to devote to their cases. It's human nature for him to feel a greater inclination to serve paying clients, and they will certainly come ahead of a client who is trying to avoid or delay payment of the fee. If you have money problems, discuss them with him and work out some kind of payment plan. He'll be more concerned about your life.

Finally, tell your attorney what you want. Don't let him guess what your goals are. Try not to talk in vague generalities—it's not enough to tell your lawyer that you want some child support, a little bit of alimony, and part of the personal property. While lawyers appreciate a free hand in negotiations and in carrying out their legal responsibilities, they still must know exactly where they're heading and what makes you happy. For example, you certainly would not want your lawyer to be spending all his time battling your husband's lawyer to obtain alimony for you when you intend to marry your boyfriend as soon as your divorce is final. If your lawyer is unaware of your post-divorce wedding plans, he may be battling to win alimony you'll never see because of your remarriage.

Chapter 9
DIVORCE: WHOSE FAULT OR NO FAULT?

We are living at a time when blame is avoided like the plague. The concept of fault is becoming more and more alien to our society. Fault implies a code of morals, wrongdoing, guilt, none of which is looked upon with favor today. More and more people are seeking to avoid responsibility for their actions, and many of them turn to the concept of "no fault." When there's a minor auto collision, it no longer matters who crossed the center line; both are paid for injuries, and dispute over who caused the accident is avoided. Many states now have no-fault insurance to settle small accident claims.

No-fault reformers have turned their attention to the matrimonial field and suggest that marriage should be allowed to end without the bitter and divisive battle over who's to blame for the breakdown. By eliminating name-calling and by keeping the dirty linen inside the marital hamper, it is supposed that everyone will be spared needless devastation in the courtroom. If the marriage is dead, the theory goes, what's the purpose of dissecting the corpse?

The primary idea behind a no-fault divorce is the recognition that neither party is blameless. If a husband is an abusive, philandering drunkard, he may explain his conduct as a result of living with an evil, corrupt woman who forced him out of the house into a self-destructive life. If a political leader is burdened with an alcoholic wife, her side of the story often is that of a wonderful, loving wife turned to the bottle by her campaigning husband who turned to his adoring campaign aides year after year. Fault? Where does it end, and where does it begin? There are no winners or losers; the only loss is the marriage.

Typical no-fault terminology for dissolving a marriage is *The marriage is irretrievably broken* (Arizona, Connecticut, Delaware, Florida, Georgia, Hawaii, Indiana, Kentucky, Massachusetts, Minnesota, Missouri, Montana, Nebraska, Washington, and Wisconsin); or *Irreconcilable differences which cause irremediable breakdown of the marriage* (California, Idaho, Maine, Mississippi, Nevada, New Hampshire, North Dakota, Oregon, Rhode Island, Tennessee, West Virginia, and Wyoming). There is also the quasi no-fault ground which allows for a divorce after both parties have voluntarily lived apart for a certain period of time (District of Columbia, Louisiana, Maryland, New Jersey, New York, North Carolina, Rhode Island, Texas, Virginia, and West Virginia). Iowa, Michigan, Texas, and the Virgin Islands permit a dissolution of the marriage when the marriage relationship has broken down to the extent that *The legitimate objects of matrimony have been destroyed, and there remains no reasonable likelihood that the relationship can be preserved.* Kansas, Oklahoma, and New Mexico allow a divorce on the ground of *incompatibility*. All of these "no-fault" states permit divorce on similarly worded and somewhat vague grounds which all have one thing in common: the parties want out.

THE EFFECT OF NO-FAULT DIVORCE ON ALIMONY

Theoretically, no-fault divorce should have no effect on whether or not a wife gets alimony. If one's right to receive alimony depends on such factors as the length of the marriage, the economic condition of the spouses, their age and health, their needs, education and potential employment opportunities, then responsibility for the marriage breakup should be immaterial. Yet the no-fault concept has a definite effect on alimony. In a fault state, a judge finds it difficult to shut his eyes to the realities of the case and ignore wrongdoing in the marriage breakup. For instance, if the wife brings proof into the courtroom that her husband beat her, committed adultery, embarrassed, humiliated, and abused her in public and, all in all, was a despicable human being, the judge might find it hard to overlook these facts when the husband's attorney rationally points out that alimony is not warranted because the wife works and makes a decent living without his help. In fact, the laws of many states still specifically link alimony with fault. So if a wife is found guilty of misconduct, many states deny her alimony. Other states permit the court to consider a husband's misconduct in awarding a wife alimony. If no-fault laws are enacted in such states, a spouse's misconduct would be irrelevant, and alimony could be awarded where ordinarily it might not be and not awarded where it might usually be given.

By eliminating fault as a ground for divorce, the responsibility on the part of the marriage partners to live up to their vows of marriage is weakened. And with the no-fault approach to divorce, it will naturally follow that a wife will have one less card to play in her attempt to either hold on to her marriage or to provide for herself after the breakup. Requiring fault to justify a divorce gives the wife an extra bargaining edge in the total framework of negotiations. She certainly needs this extra edge if her case fits the common pattern of a wife with no financial resources, whose husband controls the purse strings. In the standard case, the wife is at home attending to the cleaning, cooking, and children while the husband is out making the money and having fun. When the day of reckoning comes, he certainly would prefer a no-fault set of rules which allows him to say to his wife, "You can complain about me all you want, but the judge won't listen because we live in a no-fault state." Only *irreconcilable differences, irretrievable breakdown,* or *incompatibility* need be shown for a divorce. As for alimony, in a no-fault divorce the cold, bare, economic reality is presented to the judge; he'll never hear of the plaintiff being a battered wife, the defendant being a child abuser, or any other damaging information that makes today's practice of matrimonial law so challenging. In no-fault states, a divorce will usually be quickly and mechanically granted without emotion, trauma, accusation, and need to prove wrongdoing. The marriage partners view each other in a less vengeful manner. Their "no responsibility" attitude often extends to the financial aspects of the proceeding. The husband can rationalize, "If I'm not to blame for the marriage failure, why should I pay my ex-wife support?" No fault, no responsibility, no alimony! There also seems to be less guilt about the divorce when it is no-fault. When wrongdoing plays a role in divorce, the guilty party may be filled with remorse. When a husband deserts a faithful wife, he may be pleased to pay alimony to alleviate guilt. When abandonment as a ground for divorce is replaced with "irretrievable breakdown," guilt may vanish. Hence, the no-fault process can have the effect of reducing a spouse's chance to receive alimony.

However, a no-fault divorce does not always guarantee a compatible, easy end to a marriage. Lawyers and judges still have to grapple over key issues, such as what's best for the children, custody, child support, alimony, division of property, and other such concrete issues which have nothing to do with fault.

While more and more states are considering no-fault divorces which eliminate the requirement of proving misconduct, many states still consider fault-finding essential to the granting of a divorce.

In fact, it wasn't too long ago when adultery was the only ground for divorce in most states. In England, through the centuries, adultery was the *only* cause for divorce. Early civil law in Roman times did allow divorce on many grounds, including "If a wife goes to the theatre or the public games, without the knowledge and consent of the husband." While this ancient ground for divorce may evoke a chuckle, chauvinism is still the bottom line of marital life in most societies today. For instance, Islamic law gives the husband much greater legal status than a wife—or a woman, for that matter. The traditional Moslem divorce simply requires the husband to repudiate his wife by repeating three times, "I divorce you." This custom definitely favors the husband as the wife does not share it at all. Yet, even Moslem nations are not immune from the Women's Movement. Legislation has been proposed in many nations, including Egypt, and Turkey, to widen a Moslem woman's rights in terminating a marriage.

While a Moslem wife could rightfully complain that "Divorce comes too easily to my husband's lips," there don't seem to be any statistics to show whether the divorce rate is higher in Moslem countries than in our

81

own. It's hard to come to any definitive conclusions because there are many other factors which affect any such statistical evaluation. For example, one deterrent to divorce under Moslem law is the custom regarding a dowry. It's Moslem tradition that a man pay the dowry—but not all of it—in advance of the marriage. A stipulated sum is withheld as "spousal maintenance" for the wife in case of divorce. So she receives what might be called "a lump sum alimony payment" if her husband decides to divorce her. This could also be likened to a prenuptial contractual agreement.

Every society treats divorce in a way which fits its own beliefs and customs. Divorce is quite rare among Bedouin tribes. If a husband repudiates his wife, her male relatives will want to know why, and, depending on the misconduct of the spouses, they will kill either the wife or husband. This certainly makes many Bedouin husbands think twice before speaking thrice!

The grounds for divorce in America range from the more typical ones like cruel and inhuman treatment, habitual drunkenness, incurable insanity, desertion and abandonment, to the more unusual ones such as Illinois's ground of "attempt on life of spouse by poisoning or other means showing malice," North Carolina's ground of "bestiality," Puerto Rico's ground of "attempt of the husband or wife to corrupt their sons or prostitute their daughters and connivance in such corruption or prostitution," and Virginia's ground of "sodomy or buggery committed outside marriage." Depending on the imagination and creativity of a state's legislators, grounds for divorce can range from one simple reason to a multitude of causes. For example, Georgia spells out thirteen detailed, complex grounds for divorce, while Washington permits a marriage to be dissolved on the basis of only one.

Whatever the ground may be, those states which still require misconduct on the part of a spouse believe a marriage should not end at the whim of either partner. But many Americans today consider marriage and divorce personal matters not to be questioned by the general community. Personal rights and the right of a state to regulate the morals of its society have always been in conflict. A strong society wants to keep its control over the marriage institution, but individual rights are becoming paramount throughout the United States, and the no-fault concept has taken hold to the extent that the mere filing of divorce papers guarantees a quick end to a marriage in most states. The trend is unmistakable: no-fault is moving in, and wrongdoing is on the way out.

Chapter 10
THE
DIVORCE BATTLE
AND ALIMONY

The core of our legal process is the adversary system:
Two lawyers battle it out, and somehow justice is supposed to emerge triumphant. Justice is what our legal
system is all about; it means simply that people get what
they deserve. Unfortunately, this does not always hap-
pen. Once you accept this, you can approach your alimony problem in a more productive way. You have to
take every step you can to achieve the best result possible.
If you're lucky, you might get what you deserve.

That's where the adversary system comes in. The
theory is that if both lawyers argue their clients' causes
from opposite ends, they will somehow meet at some
reasonable middle ground where the truth lies. Yet, of
all kinds of legal proceedings, the matrimonial case is
least suited to an adversarial approach. When deciding
such issues as custody, visitation rights and support, the
lawyer with the best Perry Mason techniques should not
prevail. Rather, counsel for both sides should sit down
and, with the guidance of the court, achieve the best
possible living arrangement for the family being ripped

apart. This is essential, for there is no such thing as a weak case or a strong case when children and parents are involved.

Sure cases have often been lost in court, and the weakest of cases can be a winner. The wrong judge, the right lawyer, the convincing client, a good or bad jury— these and many other human factors make it impossible to predict a result. Rather than take chances with the legal system, most lawyers and their clients opt for an out-of-court marital settlement. Nevertheless, there are deep and legitimate differences to be resolved in any marital breakup, and a court battle is often the only way to reach a solution.

In many divorce battles, clients make their lawyers, the judge, or the legal system the scapegoat of their frustrations. When negotiations break down, when a demand or offer is outrageous, when the courts keep granting adjournment after adjournment, or when court orders are not complied with, frequently the real cause is one of the spouses and not their lawyers and the legal system. For example, if a client seeks to avoid family responsibility and takes advantage of legal procedures to introduce delays into the proceeding, the legal system may appear to be at fault when in fact it is doing exactly as it is supposed to do; it cannot ignore dilatory tactics if they are legal procedures.

TEMPORARY DIVORCE INSANITY

In many divorce battles, it's not unusual for a client to report to the lawyer that the other spouse is "crazy." A husband will tell his lawyer that his wife's insanity is the reason why the divorce is so difficult. Subconsciously, he also may be justifying why he could not live with his wife any longer. Strangely enough, wives don't usually accuse husbands of being insane; for some reason, they prefer to describe husbands as "sick." There is a subtle distinction. When a husband says his wife is insane, he truly believes it and is quite certain the condition is incurable. That's why his marriage can't be saved. But when a wife calls her husband sick, she really still loves him and believes his condition is curable. Her hope is that as soon as he regains his mental health, he will realize what he is throwing away and will return to her begging forgiveness. Too often, wives label husbands "sick" when they have fallen head over heels for a much younger woman. In their opinion, such conduct can only be described as "sick."

No matter what spouses call each other, the simple fact is that a divorce proceeding is one of the most emotional and traumatic ones in the legal system, and it is, therefore, not unusual for one or both of the parties to go through periods of deep depression, perhaps even consider suicide. The tearing asunder of a once loving family means that family members lose all perspective on their lives and the world around them. Their conduct and judgments are irrational. They may become paranoid, depressed, and lethargic. This condition has been diagnosed as TDI: Temporary Divorce Insanity and is the reason why many lawyers would prefer to handle an estate, real estate closing, or car accident case, and why most judges would rather hear a car accident case or a malpractice suit than preside over a marital dispute. Perhaps it's natural to shy away from another's family problems, but such an attitude in the legal system makes the practice of matrimonial law extremely difficult. This climate of reluctance hampers efforts to help battling couples work out their problems. Few matters deserve greater attention in our society than cries for help from a faltering family unit, yet these cries often get short shrift in our system of justice.

Because of this attitude, lawyers always try to work out the marital differences without going to court. In fact, most matrimonial actions are settled before they get into the courtroom.

Negotiations to settle marital disputes boil down to hard bargaining, haggling, and even bartering. "If you take less alimony, I'll give you extra child support," or "You take our girl, and I'll take our boy," or "I'll sign the house over to you, and you drop your claim for alimony." These are some of the many points to be hammered out in a divorce settlement. In negotiations, it's not unusual for the issues to become linked or dependent on each other. You give something to get something; that's the way in which every separation agreement is worked out and every divorce reaches its conclusion. Life insurance, medical payments, alimony, child support, the house, custody, visitation, estate rights, division of personal property, automobile—all go into the total package of ending a marriage. Couples are often woefully ignorant about just how much has to be done to return them to an unmarried state.

In the battle to get the best terms, alimony is just one issue. Winning or losing the issue depends on who wants what badly enough. If a husband wants out and his wife doesn't, if he feels guilty and she feels injured, and if he has a weak lawyer and she has a hard-nosed, courtroom "killer," then clearly he is going to end up paying alimony. The wife has all the cards and the right lawyer to play them. If the facts are reversed—a husband with no desire to end the marriage, a top attorney, and a wife who wants out—then he may escape without having to pay alimony. The most ironic observation with each of these situations, however, is that the economic status of the couple, their financial needs, and the question of what is equitable and fair has little bearing on the results.

As the swords are drawn in an alimony battle, there is always the possibility that extreme demands can prevent a reasonable compromise settlement. While it's common knowledge and accepted negotiation tactics that both parties offer and demand sums that are much higher or lower, as the case may be, than they are finally willing to accept, those sums should be kept within reason. Otherwise, if a husband offers his wife alimony that is ridiculously inadequate, he leaves her no choice but to take extreme legal measures rather then negotiate. Likewise, if the wife demands alimony far above the reasonable level, the husband feels justified in resorting to evasion of all support obligations. Many a wife has upped her demands in such unreasonable fashion that the husband has been forced to go bankrupt, sell his business, move away, or quit his job, leaving her with little or no recourse for alimony. Many spouses who could have negotiated a fair financial settlement early on ruin that possibility when they refuse to consider any reasonable offer from their mate. There is a fine line between tough but acceptable bargaining positions and extreme positions, which turn good faith negotiations into bitter and self-destructive behavior.

ESTHER AND JOE HINES

Joe Hines was loved by everybody. Over a period of forty years, he worked his way up from apprentice carpenter to a city building inspector and, finally, to the top post of Commissioner of Buildings. He was one of the select public officials who got his job on merit. He managed to avoid political entanglements throughout the years, and while never endearing himself to any Mayor, he had the respect and support of all of them. One basis for that respect was his personal life. A regular churchgoer, Joe was never seen without his wife, Esther. Joe had never known another woman. Joe and Esther grew up on the same block, became childhood friends, then sweethearts, and were married when each was only nineteen. It was considered an ideal marriage. Joe never did anything without consulting Esther, and he never spent a night away from home without her. Whenever he went on a business trip or to a professional convention, Esther accompanied him. She was as well known and well liked as Joe. No one knew why they were childless, although their friends often speculated. The most common opinion was that they were unable to have children and preferred not to adopt. Very few would have guessed that they had made a decision early in their marriage to live with and for each other without the responsibilities of a family. Both had known poverty and had watched their own parents struggle to provide for them. Joe and Esther agreed they did not want to continue that struggle.

Divorce was something to which the Hineses paid scant attention; in fact, they were shocked when they discovered friends breaking up. Like any couple, Joe and Esther had their tough times and fair share of heartaches; both were affected by change of life, which severely strained their usually content home atmosphere.

The first real wedge, which was to open a chasm of marital discord, began with Esther's annual checkup a week before their thirty-ninth wedding anniversary. When Joe came home that night, he found her distraught. The doctor had discovered suspicious lumps on several parts of Esther's body and wanted her to enter the hospital the next day. The operation was a total success; despite the doctor's reassurances, however, Esther was convinced she had no more than six months to live. A crisis such as this often strengthens marriages, but in this case it drove Joe and Esther apart. The more Joe attempted to comfort and sustain his wife, the more she repelled him and claimed he no longer loved her. She became paranoid when he was away from home; in time, her attitude finally alienated him from her altogether.

While Esther's lumps were malignant, the doctors were confident they had removed all the cancerous tissue. Her chances for survival were excellent. But if her physical condition offered a good prognosis, her emotional condition did not. She had always felt secure and confident. She was proud to be Joe Hines's wife and always considered herself an asset to his life, professionally and socially. They had always been partners and fully met each other's needs. Overnight this self-image changed, and she began to think of herself as a dying woman and therefore a hindrance to Joe. She convinced herself that he no longer loved her. The harder he tried, the more she felt his efforts were insincere. Her fears were soon realized. Joe could no longer act naturally toward her as in the past; rather he was always trying to please her and prove he really loved and needed her. In a desperate move to save their relationship, Joe considered early retirement so that he could spend more time with her. When he broached the idea, Esther became hysterical and said that he must have found out from the doctor that she had little time left to live. She wouldn't hear of his retirement although she did agree to his taking a one-month leave of absence. They traveled to Europe, but the trip turned out to be a fiasco. They never stopped bickering.

Where once they could never find anything to disagree about, there was now hardly a matter that didn't cause conflict. After two years, Joe, with great reluctance, went to a divorce lawyer. Esther's only comment was that she was not surprised because she knew he stopped loving her when he found out she was dying. Esther's lawyer found her a bitter woman who demanded that he use any means to get every penny out of Joe. Joe's lawyer found a client who was full of sorrow over what had been lost, a client who had no fight in him and no desire to deny any demand his wife made—not an easy attitude to maintain, given Esther's performance. Whenever one demand was met, a new and more unreasonable one was raised. The only two issues to be resolved were how to divide their property and what kind of support should go to Esther. Esther believed all of the property, including the house, should go to her and that Joe should leave with nothing but his clothing. Joe didn't fight this to any great length, but there were some items of personal property that he refused to give up: his grandfather's rifle, his coin collection (which Esther had never really liked because she felt it took so much time away from her throughout their marriage), his tools and workbench and finally, his proudest accomplishment, the oak desk he built before their marriage. However, Esther demanded all of these, and nothing would change her mind. As for alimony, this too became an irreconcilable conflict. No matter what Joe offered, Esther responded that it wasn't enough. As she didn't think she was going to live too long, she felt that there was no amount large enough that Joe could pay her. They were in and out of courts to no avail. Finally, Joe retired and moved south. Esther spent the remaining years of her life going from lawyer to lawyer, carrying a thick briefcase filled with legal papers. She never stopped complaining about the lack of justice in the courts. When she died at age 63, it was from natural causes; it could be said, however, that she committed emotional suicide. Joe died shortly thereafter, brokenhearted over a good life gone inexplicably sour and empty.

Of all the issues battled in court, alimony is often the most difficult to resolve. A contested alimony case can bring out the worst kinds of tirades between spouses, for example:

Stock-in-Trade Legal Quotes From Attorney Seeking Alimony for Wife

1. "She spent all her life raising the family; she doesn't know how to do anything else."
2. "How can she make a living? She's always been a mother."
3. "He's made her a nervous wreck, and now he should pay for it!"
4. "My client has always been totally dependent on him, and she can't survive now without his help."
5. "She gave him the best years of her life, and now he throws her out like a piece of garbage."

6. "If he wants out—let him pay for it!"
7. "She just can't afford to live without his help."
8. "She gave her life up for him, and now what does she have to show for it?"
9. "If it wasn't for her, he wouldn't have amounted to anything in life."

Stock-in-Trade Legal Quotes From Attorney Fighting Alimony on Behalf of Husband

1. "She has a college education just like he does, so let her support herself!"
2. "Let her get a job like everyone else!"
3. "My client can't afford to give her a penny."
4. "The way she turned the kids against him—she doesn't deserve one red nickel."
5. "The way she's treated him throughout the marriage—he won't give her one dime."
6. "She always threw Women's Lib in his face—now she can be liberated! She can support herself!"
7. "She's not going to live off him the rest of her life!"
8. "She can always get a job as a maid."
9. "Without her around, he could have made something of his life."

A common plea in an alimony dispute is "Look at all I've given to this marriage." Sometimes a distraught wife will beg the court for alimony with the declaration that she has given her husband "the best years of her life." She concludes her tirade with "And what do I have to show for it?" or "Now, I'm left with absolutely nothing." The husband's answer is usually equally outrageous. The best of his worst replies is frequently: "What do you mean, I gave you nothing; you used to like it when we were first married."

This notion of giving and receiving in marriage or,

in fact, in any loving relationship, is not really a valid one. Couples who live together, whether married or unmarried, do not keep track of everything they give and receive. The relationship should be a concept of sharing, loving, fulfilling needs, and helping each other to grow and be better people. There is no dollar value on five years of marriage. Yet assessing value is exactly what lawyers and judges are forced to do in alimony cases. Generally speaking, alimony is awarded in matrimonial actions at the court's discretion. As a rule of thumb, it should be awarded where "justice requires" based on several factors, including the length of the marriage, the ability of the wife or the husband to be self-supporting, and the contributions made by the spouses to the marital assets. No matter how it's defined or described and no matter what standards or factors are used at arriving at it, alimony is most often viewed in terms of need above all else. This attitude often leads to unjust results.

FAMILY COURT

Few matrimonial disputes can avoid Family Court. The first symptoms of marriage failure usually show up there. And for most divorcing couples, their local Family Court represents all that is traumatic and frustrating in the unhappy days of their marriage termination. Family Courts are a crowded battleground for all sorts of marital disputes, and any lawyers or clients who understand the psychology and nature of the Court can count themselves very fortunate. It is human nature to seek an easy way out; this rule of life applies in Family Court. Judges, lawyers, and court personnel look for the quickest and easiest way through the immense caseload.

There are a number of ways to avoid bitter, time-consuming litigation. The most useful and commonly used tool is the adjournment, which means delay. That almost always suits one side of a family dispute, usually the side that holds all the cards. If, for example, in a child custody proceeding, the husband wants custody of his children or visitation rights, the wife has the advantage—the children. The more delay she can get in the proceeding, the better off she will be. Why? The more the children are with her, the less the chance that a judge will remove them from their familiar environment. The children will be established in school and entrenched in the neighborhood, church and city programs; when the case finally gets to the judge months or even years later, he may be more than reluctant to take them away from their friends and stable environment. Such delays also serve to depress the father, who is losing time and money with each adjournment. The wife hopes he'll give up the fight eventually.

The tables are turned when a wife is seeking support for herself or the children. The cards are now in the hands of the husband for he has the money. The more delay he can obtain, the better off he will be. Why? The longer he holds onto the money, the harder it will be for his family to survive without his wife finding alternative ways to support them. The wife may move in with her parents instead of getting her own apartment. She may find a part-time job. When they finally get to court, the judge may conclude she doesn't need much; after all, she managed for the past five months without any of his money. More likely, the wife will ease her demands and accept less than she wants—maybe less than she deserves—to end the constant aggravation and uncertainty.

There is an art to obtaining a court adjournment. Some lawyers know at least fifty ways to leave a judge—without having the case heard. To list only a few:

1. "My client suddenly got ill."
2. "My key witness is not available."

3. "One of the children is sick, and my client couldn't get a babysitter."
4. "My client is having a nervous breakdown." (This excuse is usually valid.)
5. "Your Honor, we will need an interpreter as my client does not speak English..." and "It may take some weeks to find a Croatian interpreter."

Or the lawyer can send his client in to say:

6. "My lawyer is out of town."
7. "My lawyer is on vacation."
8. "My lawyer is sick."
9. "My lawyer is in another court."
10. "My lawyer didn't schedule this on his diary and can't be reached."
11. "My lawyer has a dentist appointment."

In terms of legal gamesmanship, there are also ways for a lawyer to seek an adjournment:

12. Ask the judge to disqualify himself because he knows the father of the wife, he had his car repaired at the husband's uncle's garage, etc., any of which will cause the judge to take time to think about it.
13. Make a motion that the court does not have jurisdiction to hear the matter. He'll get at least ten days to submit legal memorandums to support your position and then another two weeks' extension when his secretary gets sick and can't type the papers.
14. Move for a change of venue because one of the parties moved out of town.

Whatever the excuse, Family Court is notorious for having cases postponed. Underlying these continual delays is the hope that the problem will somehow disappear or be worked out. In fact, Family Court is not in the business of either saving or ending marriages. Rather it serves as a way station along the divorce route to resolve temporarily the immediate needs of a battling couple. Spouses run to this court in emergency situations. They need money to eat, they want to see their kids, they want the judge to tell an abusing spouse to keep his hands off the rest of the family. The very basic problems of a family run amuck are handled by this court, but it rarely provides the final solution for a marital dispute. It does serve as a stopgap until the lawyers can negotiate a settlement. The fact is that most marital differences are resolved in the lawyer's office and not in a courtroom. If they are not, the first courtroom seen by a fighting couple is invariably the Family Court.

Chapter 11
ALIMONY: A METHOD TO RESTORE ECONOMIC BALANCE

While alimony is losing its validity as a form of penalty, revenge, or lifetime support for a spouse, it still can serve a legitimate purpose. The following situations are just a few examples.

#1

A husband takes the earnings and inheritance of his wife and pours it into his business. A divorce follows. Equity clearly demands that the husband allow his wife to share in the benefits of her own money. A classic case would be where a husband uses his wife's $25,000 trust fund to start "his" business and then seeks a divorce six years later. He claims she's still young and healthy and can go out and make her own living. She replies that his net income of $45,000 a year comes out of a business that was created with her grandfather's money, and she wants either a fair share of the business or reimbursement—plus interest—for what she has put into it.

#2

A wife supports her husband so he can achieve his career goals. She willingly delays implementing her own plans. When her husband succeeds, he loses interest in her or feels he's outgrown her and so asks for a divorce, and contends she now needs less money because she has only herself to support! She alleges "chutzpah" and wants financial support from him so she can now achieve her own career goals.

#3

A couple lives together through a long and prosperous marriage in which the wife is dependent on the husband in all respects. After 30 years, however, things turn sour, and the husband wants a divorce. The wife has no ability to earn money and is in poor health. She wants her husband to give her weekly alimony payments because she hasn't the emotional, physical, or educational resources to make it on her own.

#4

For 20 years, a wife handles all household chores, the raising of four children, and total management of the home. This frees her husband to spend all of his time building a business. By the time the marriage falters, he has accumulated great wealth—the tangible results of his efforts—while the wife has produced very different results: four outstanding young adults and her husband's success. If this couple and their marriage are viewed in a total context, then his wealth may be directly attributable to her efforts, as well as his. If raising and caring for the family are equally his responsibility and he relinquished it all to his wife, then equity may require this factor as a consideration when dividing up their property.

#5

Many husbands and wives work together in a family business. The wife feeds the children, bundles them off to school, cleans the house, and works with her husband to build a fledgling business into a large, successful enterprise. During the early years, she plays an indispensable business role, sharing business decisions, policy judgments, and the everyday chores, including unpacking cartons, keeping inventory, making sales, and sweeping the floor. Years later, when the marriage breaks down, her role in the business has diminished to bookkeeper and gal Friday, as far as the other twelve employees are concerned. Of course, the twelve were not there during the embryo years, so none can appreciate the significant contributions she has made to her husband's business. When the time for divorce arrives, the husband argues that it's his business, and she is entitled to nothing. He's trying to "give her the business" by not giving her anything! In such a situation, alimony may be justified as the only way the wife can obtain her rightful slice of the economic pie.

ERICA AND HOWARD

Erica and Howard met during their first year at college and decided to get married at graduation four years later. They would have tied the knot sooner except that they had no money, and in deference to both their parents' wishes, they waited. It was always understood that Howard would go on to law school to fulfill his lifelong ambition to be a lawyer, and that Erica would, for the time being, put aside her interest in a medical career so she could pay his expenses at law school. Between her full-time secretarial job, his summer employment, and an annual student loan, they managed to meet the demands of tuition and inflation.

No one was prouder than Erica when Howard graduated with honors; therefore, it certainly came as a shock when Howard told her one month later he no longer loved her and wanted a divorce. After the initial pain subsided, Erica realized that Howard's explanation that he had "outgrown her" was false. The truth was that Howard's law study group of six fellow students included one "fellow" named Sheila, a striking and brilliant young woman who had caught Howard's fancy. Erica was too naïve and too in love to have been suspicious of Howard's many late night study sessions.

Not only did Howard want a divorce, he also considered himself a legal beagle determined to invoke the principles of ERA to explain away his obligations to Erica. As he told her, "You're a big girl, and there's no reason why you can't now support yourself. It would certainly be easier than the burden of taking care of the two of us." When she reminded him of her desire to be a doctor, he sincerely wished her luck but offered nothing. His law school studies had shown him that a short marriage without children and with a healthy wife who was already working would never warrant alimony. What his studies did not teach him to evaluate was the anger of a woman who felt used. She had no intention of being tossed aside without some reimbursement for supporting him through law school. The matter never got to trial because Erica's lawyer convinced Howard's attorney that fairness and equity clearly dictated some lump sum payment to Erica, so that she might quit her job and go to medical school. Howard finally agreed to pay $10,000 toward her medical education. Since he was just a fledgling attorney, he could only pay her on a weekly installment basis. Erica agreed to accept this $10,000 in 100 weekly payments at $100 per week.

Because the installment payments ended within approximately two years, the payments did not constitute alimony for tax purposes, and Erica did not have to pay income tax on them. Howard, however, was not able to claim a deduction. He had been under the impression that alimony was tax deductible, so it came as quite a shock to him that he lost this tax benefit in his settlement. Perhaps he had missed class on the day alimony and taxes were discussed, or maybe he had the wrong lawyer representing him—the brilliant and striking Sheila!

WHEN ALIMONY IS NOT ENOUGH

Horror stories about the poor people who pay exorbitant alimony abound. A frequent comment from observers of such situations is that alimony shouldn't be awarded or that it is too high. Few realize that there are situations where no amount of alimony can adequately protect some wives. A classic case would be a long marriage brought to a sudden end by a restless husband. The couple is in their sixties, but the husband looks and feels forty-five, while his wife looks and acts seventy. Forty years of marriage proved a heavy drain on her, what with the bearing and raising of five children, while he has thrived and kept himself young, thanks to his exciting and dynamic business life. Now he's worth millions; as far as he's concerned, his wife is worthless. He wants to live vigorously to the end, and she is no longer his fit companion.

The first misstatement is the husband's belief that "he" is worth millions, when in fact "they" are worth millions. His second mistake is to assume that she should be happy with a very substantial weekly alimony payment. Her lawyer first has to convince her and then has to convince the husband's lawyer that no amount of weekly alimony can adequately protect her for her remaining years. What this wife and so many others don't immediately realize is that their most important asset at this point in life is their right of survivorship as surviving spouses. If a husband drops dead in the middle of divorce negotiations (at 69, this hyperkinetic male was a definite risk), she would automatically be entitled to one-third of his estate under her state's estate law. Since he is worth approximately $6,000,000, his predivorce death would bring her about $2,000,000. Not an inconsequential sum to make secure her later years. And no one could argue that she didn't deserve this kind of financial security after sharing forty years of an often difficult life with her demanding spouse. On the other hand, if she agrees to accept the sum of $2,000-a-week alimony and he drops dead one day after the divorce, she would not receive one penny from his estate for the rest of her life, assuming he died before the first alimony payment was made. It would be unwise for her attorney to merely settle for a weekly alimony payment no matter how substantial it was. Instead, there is a far more equitable way of settling such a dispute as is illustrated by the following case.

103

JAY AND YVETTE BEVINS

When Jay Bevins asked his wife for a divorce, she thought he was kidding. After thirty-four years of marriage, Yvette and Jay had a comfortable relationship. Jay always appeared totally pleased with his family, his business, and his life. Mild-mannered in the tradition of Clark Kent, Jay was the epitome of courtliness. However, like Clark Kent, Jay had a secret side to his character. While he could not leap large buildings in a single bound, he did make great strides for any pretty young woman in distress—or otherwise.

Over the years, his dalliances were superficial and shortlived—until he met Lisa. When he decided to leave Yvette for Lisa, he had no intention of abandoning his wife financially. He instructed his lawyer to approach the divorce negotiations in a most generous manner. He had no intention of depriving Yvette of a fair financial settlement. As for Yvette, she wisely instructed her lawyer to make certain that she obtained the most generous financial settlement possible to protect her in her remaining years. At age 62, after thirty-four years of marriage, she had no intention of watching Lisa walk away with Jay's money, while she was left with a pittance.

Both sides arrived at a twenty-four page separation agreement loaded with financial terms favoring Yvette. Most important of all was a paragraph which provided that Jay would write his will and therein leave Yvette one-third of his estate. This provision was quite complicated because it contained conditions which were designed to prevent Jay from changing his will after the divorce or from depleting his estate before his death. The separation agreement was drafted very carefully and was made as ironclad as possible; for it was anticipated that when Jay died, Lisa, as his surviving spouse, would not view with favor a will which gave one third of Jay's estate to his ex-wife.

Sure enough, when Jay died eight years after the divorce, Lisa instructed the estate lawyers not to honor either the separation agreement or Jay's will. Lisa's attorneys advised her that she was wasting her money because she would lose, but Lisa didn't care. The main purpose of her lawsuit was spiteful: to prevent Yvette from sharing in the estate as long as possible. The legal battle waged in the lower and upper Appeals Courts took two years. As predicted, Yvette prevailed and received one third of Jay's estate with interest from the time of his death. When the final estate figures were in, Yvette received $240,000, Jay and Yvette's children $385,000, Lisa $185,000, and the estate attorneys $47,000.

If Yvette had failed to receive this kind of estate protection at the time of the divorce, she would have received alimony for only eight years. She would then have had to live off Social Security, while Lisa inherited the bulk of Jay's money.

ALIMONY WITHOUT END

Ben Franklin noted that the only two certainties in life are death and taxes. Alimony may even continue after death, however. Probate courts have often ruled that an estate must pay alimony to the former wife of a decedent until she either dies or remarries.

BILL AND TILLIE MARTIN

When Bill Martin decided to end his 33-year marriage, he did so with both sadness and reluctance. He cared deeply for his wife, Tillie. They didn't have a perfect union, but it lasted long enough for them to successfully raise their four children and for him to establish a thriving mattress factory.

Bill always had an eye for a pretty woman, and he finally decided to shed his faithful wife so he could play the field without guilt. By now the children were grown and could better cope with their parents' divorce. He had every intention of providing for Tillie for the rest of her life. Once they resolved the financial aspect of the divorce, Bill could move on to his new life. Tillie had no desire to fight and, in fact, would have done anything to please Bill. She still loved him and hoped that he would come to his senses, even after the divorce. She quickly accepted his first offer to give her $200-a-week alimony, knowing he would treat her fairly and would give her no more and no less than he could live with. At the time of the divorce, Bill Martin said under oath in court that he would make the payments of $200 a week "for the rest of her life."

Bill died three months after the divorce. He never had a chance to begin his new life and, as far as Tillie was concerned, he certainly did not have enough time to come to his senses and return to her. She immediately took over the funeral arrangements as the bereaved widow, and no one among the family or friends objected. Everyone strongly felt it was the right thing. The brief span between the divorce and his death was treated as if it hadn't really existed. Unfortunately for Tillie, this "glossing over" could not be continued once the lawyers began to handle Bill's estate. They could not overlook the fact that Tillie was not his wife at the time of his death and so could not be treated as a surviving spouse. She was therefore not entitled to a widow's share of Bill's substantial $500,000 estate. Even more appalling to Tillie was the fact that Bill's will, though unchanged from before the divorce, was totally ineffective as it related to her. His will had given his entire estate to her, but this will was revoked by New York law, which specifically states that a divorce between spouses automatically revokes any bequest made to the other spouse in a will drawn before the divorce.

What hurt Tillie most was the discovery that her $200-a-week alimony payment stopped the day Bill died. When she called the estate lawyers to ask why the weekly money was not being sent to her, she expected some reasonable explanation such as, "It will take time for the estate to be sorted out" or "We need court approval to make the payments." Instead, the estate lawyers had the sad task of advising her that under New York State law, alimony payments cease when the paying spouse dies. Tillie immediately hired her own lawyer to get what was rightfully hers. After researching the case, he reluctantly advised her not to waste her time or money in legal proceedings. While it was true that Bill had stated orally in open court that he would make the payments "for the rest of her life," New York clearly held that an oral statement in court was not binding on the estate. She could have protected herself at the time of the divorce by having a written separation agreement drawn up which specifically provided for her $200-a-week-alimony payment to continue after his death for as long as she lived. Unfortunately, Tillie had not concerned herself about her rights at the time of the divorce. She had just wanted to please Bill and make everything easy for him. He had always taken care of her in the past, and she had faith that he would do so at the time of the divorce. Things did not work out that way. Instead, Bill's entire estate passed to his four children and, fortunately for Tillie, they voluntarily assumed the responsibility of supporting their mother for her remaining years.

While alimony can extend beyond death, the terms of the financial arrangement must be spelled out in writing if it is to be upheld by the courts. If nothing is said to the contrary, alimony automatically ceases upon remarriage or death, death meaning the demise of either spouse.

ALIMONY FOR HUSBANDS

In the future, as more and more wives become breadwinners, more husbands may be pushed out of the job market and back into the home *or* will opt to be there. Househusbands will become more common in the '80s, and many will be there from choice and their own sense of fulfillment. Others will stay home because of unemployment, while the wife maintains her income. If that kind of family situation exists, courts may be asked to provide a husband with fair treatment when a marriage breaks up. He might seek custody, child support, and alimony. Whatever argument can be used about a wife's right to alimony can apply to a husband. Restoring economic imbalance between spouses works both ways. If the husband is at home, he might argue that he is entitled to economic support to correct the imbalance and to restore him to a position of self-sufficiency. If he is sick, unable to work or if he in some way subjugated his own economic needs and potential to meet the needs of the home and children, then he also might be entitled to alimony from his wife.

Another situation which might warrant alimony for the male is where a young man of very modest means marries a rich young woman and lives as her lover, companion, and escort without any means of support for himself. If she sheds him for another, he might well run to court for support. His case may not yet arouse much sympathy from the bench, though the reverse of this situation has often produced much compassion on the part of judges.

CAROL AND RANDY HOTALING

Carol and Randy Hotaling were high school lovers who married at age 17. After sixteen years of marriage and three children, Carol decided she had had enough. She realized she and Randy were simply too different. Furthermore, she was only 33 and felt that she still had her whole life before her. She liked to stay out late and party with her friends. Randy was a homebody who liked to help the kids with homework, read stories to them at bedtime, and then enjoy a beer and watch television. It was his idea of a perfect night. These evenings were too confining for Carol; she felt she had to get out of the house. She used any excuse to escape, and Randy never raised an eyebrow. As long as his Carol was happy, he was satisfied. So Carol bowled two nights a week, played bingo one night, and spent weekends with her two girlfriends. The more Carol was away from home, the less she wanted to return. There was no doubt she adored her children, but she did not like changing diapers, doing dishes, cooking meals, making beds or disciplining the kids. Finally, she got a full-time job as a clerical assistant at a large local factory.

From that point on, a new world was opened up to her. Her office was frequented by corporate executives and, for the first time in her life, Carol had close contact with dynamic, ambitious, and often attractive men. Shortly after she went to work, Randy was laid off from his job. Their reverse employment situation forced them to closely examine their family roles, and it was clear that Randy was as happy to be home taking care of the family as Carol was thrilled to be out in the work world. After awhile, Randy stopped going to the union hall to find employment. Carol, meanwhile, moved herself up in position and salary by taking advantage of every educational program and by showing great initiative in each of her new responsibilities.

They lived this way for six years before the inevitable happened: Carol fell in love with a vice-president of the company and asked Randy for a divorce. Randy was not surprised, but after years of raising the family, he felt justified in asking for alimony, custody, and child support. Carol was not prepared to contest the custody aspect of the case, and she was willing to pay child support, but she felt it would be degrading to herself and to Randy if she paid him alimony. When Randy's lawyers argued that alimony would be quickly given if Randy was the wife and Carol the husband, Carol's lawyers could only respond feebly, "Maybe so, but the fact remains that Randy is a man, and so he shouldn't get alimony." The issue could not be resolved and was left to the courts to decide. The judge, in a rather terse decision, held that Randy was not entitled to alimony, since there was no showing that he was ill or unable to obtain employment. The judge concluded that "The husband herein is an able-bodied American male, and he can go out and get a job like anyone else." This same judge was noted for giving generous alimony awards to wives, especially when the husbands had left to marry other women.

SOME CREATIVE WAYS TO MAKE ALIMONY FAIR AND USEFUL

The standard idea of alimony is that it's a weekly payment which continues until death or remarriage. In fact, alimony can be fitted to meet specific needs. It need not be forever; it need not be the same sum throughout the payment period; it need not cease only on remarriage or death. One reason alimony is so bitterly fought and rejected is that no one stops to look behind the payment to figure out why it is needed. Once the parties understand the purpose for alimony in their particular case, they may find it easier to reach mutually acceptable terms which can specifically fill the need but which do not scare the paying spouse into thinking that alimony is an unbearable, endless yoke.

An imaginative approach to alimony can be used in cases where a wife panics at the prospect of facing the outside world on her own. Even if she is capable of doing it, the one thing she often lacks is self-confidence. This is especially the case when a wife has spent several years raising children, with her husband serving not only as breadwinner but also as the one who happily assumed every outside chore for her and the family. She may not expect or deserve alimony from him for the remainder of her life, but she's scared, and the only help she can immediately seek is money from her husband. To ease her immediate fears and to help her stand on her own two feet, an arrangement can be made which would provide her with a high-alimony figure for the first year following the divorce. This amount could then be dramatically decreased at specified intervals and finally be eliminated after several years. This type of decreasing alimony would help the wife by giving her time to adjust to a life without her husband. It also encourages her to move out into the world and do something fulfilling, both for personal satisfaction and income, as she knows his economic support won't last forever.

A creative alimony arrangement can take the opposite approach: Increasing alimony. In a typical case, the husband, after a long marriage and several children, wants to start a new life without his wife. Her one concern is to receive substantial alimony for the rest of her life. He earns a good salary, and after twenty-six years of marriage, she knows that she now doesn't have the ability to obtain a decent job. The job market offers little for a woman of 51 who has no educational background and whose only claim to fame is serving as a faithful wife and good mother. He, on the other hand, is not adverse to paying her a good amount of alimony, but he rightfully claims that he is not able to do so at present. After all, two of their children are now in college, and the remaining three are in their expensive teen years. His immediate concern is to support the children and see to it that each one receives a complete education. Both wife and husband agree with this short-term goal, but she is personally concerned with her own long-term goals. She knows that all too soon her youngest will be grown and on his own, and she will then have to face ten, twenty, and maybe even thirty years without the pleasure of her husband's company or money. In this case, an alimony arrangement can be created where she receives a small amount at first, but one which increases as each child goes on his own. She will arrive at her highest level of alimony support when all of the children are out of the house. This financial arrangement suits her because that's when she's going to want the most alimony.

ALIMONY AND CHILD SUPPORT: TWO SEPARATE ISSUES

Many divorcing couples tend to blur alimony with child support when discussing support payments to the family. Yet, alimony and child support are different concepts based on separate legal principles and having substantially different tax and legal consequences.

Both parents have a responsibility to support their children. In determining this amount, a judge should look at the total needs and income of the family and determine how much money one or both parents can provide as a fair and reasonable amount of support for their children. Alimony does not mean support and has nothing to do with the children. It's a payment between spouses, and a judge determines this amount without relation to family needs and parental responsibilities.

Despite these differences, many couples, their lawyers, and even judges often lump child support and alimony into one figure. For example, the typical Family Court order directs that the husband "pay to his wife and three children the sum of $120 each and every week for their support." Does that mean $30-a-week support for each of the three children and $30 alimony? Does it mean $40-a-week support for each of the three children and no alimony? Or does it mean $60-a-week alimony and $20-a-week support for each of the three children? No one knows. And it's fairly obvious that the division of the total figure will make a substantial difference to each of the family members. If the couple's three children are ages 14, 16, and 18, they will soon be grown and out of the house. The husband would therefore prefer to view the $120 figure as all child support which ends as soon as the last child is emancipated. The wife would rather consider the figure as $60 alimony and $60 child support, so that she can continue to receive the $60 weekly payment long after the children are out of the house. This vital issue should not be left to be fought out at a later time in another court. Sometimes these figures are blurred because everyone is trying to avoid fighting about yet another difficult issue. Unfortunately, there's a general theory in legal practice which states, "If you can escape dealing with a difficult problem today, do so!" However, that extra effort is worth it. It's still best to do the job right the first time around and avoid expensive bitter fights later on.

Chapter 12
HIDDEN ASSETS

Even in a case where alimony is clearly warranted, the real problem remains: How much should it be? One of the key elements in determining a fair alimony payment is the financial means of the paying spouse. This is the hardest aspect of an alimony proceeding; ironically, spouses most entitled to alimony are often married to mates who are least willing to pay.

SUSAN AND TOM

In their twenty-two years of marriage, Susan never saw a checkbook, safe deposit box, teller's window, stock, or bond. Her husband Tom was the sole owner of a highly successful manufacturing firm, and he was not one to delegate any matter of importance to his wife. Nothing was more important to Tom than the operation and management of his household—that is, next to his manufacturing firm, which he had nurtured

115

from a three-man operation to one which employed 400. Susan did not object to Tom's running the household, although she was sometimes annoyed at his chauvinistic attitude toward her and their two daughters. He often spoke of one of his three sons coming into the business, but somehow he could not imagine his two daughters in the business world. Instead, they were going to marry well and make him a proud grandfather. Still, Susan loved him for what he was and was sustained by her perception of him when they first got married and were struggling at home and in his business. Unfortunately, Tom's perception of himself gradually changed with his success, until he had subconsciously reached the point of resenting Susan's somewhat stale perception of him. He found his secretary's perception of him more to his liking. Jane idolized Tom and knew him only as a dynamic, self-assured powerhouse.

After much soul-searching and agonizing, Tom decided to move out of the house to give himself a chance to sort out his emotions. Only then did Susan suddenly realize that she was in trouble. Even if she could survive the traumatic blow to her ego and the havoc wreaked on their deeply saddened and confused five children, how could she ever face the world outside after living in such a protected, sheltered environment? She did a wonderful job raising a family and running a household, but could she make it in that big scary world outside? Even if she was emotionally and psychologically prepared to make it on her own, was she educationally prepared? Susan had left college in her sophomore year to marry Tom, and now she was 41, a jilted mother of five with no college degree, no work experience, and certainly no basis for confidence in her ability to face the business world. She was in no hurry to end the marriage. She was even willing to take four or five years to come to terms with these overwhelming issues. But Tom began a divorce action only three weeks after he left the house.

In this typical case, what happens to Susan if Tom has everything in his name and has no intention of sharing "his" hard-earned assets? Even more to the point, how does she discover Tom's assets if he is determined to conceal them?

One of the most difficult aspects of determining alimony is finding out the true worth of the parties. Concealing assets is a common tool employed by spouses in contested divorces. Because of this, many states have passed laws which require spouses to give full disclosure of their finances in written affidavits, which also allow pretrial examinations of spouses. These laws attempt to reduce the element of guesswork, surprise, and outright fraud in matrimonial disputes. In fact, the trend over the years has been toward an honest and total exchange of information between the attorneys for battling spouses, so that each side can better evaluate its case and reach a more reasonable and fair settlement of their differences. If they can't work the case out between themselves, the court will have a head start by the open and full disclosure of all economic assets of the spouses. Even if the laws favor full financial disclosure, many spouses still go to great lengths to hide their assets in order to avoid or minimize alimony.

We've all heard the saying: "The richer you are, the richer you get." There's a commonly held belief that the wealthy get all the breaks, while the poor pay for it in one way or another. So the millionaire pays no taxes, and the hardworking wage earner suffers. Why should the field of alimony be any different?

Often it is not. The wealthy person forms corporations, entangling partnerships, tax shelters, and tax hideaways, and the hapless wife has difficulty getting a share of the family fortune. Many a millionaire has pleaded poverty in the alimony court, convincing the judge that although everyone thinks he's rich, it's only a paper profit which leaves him nothing to feed his wife and seven children. He does feed himself, however, since his food is a corporate expense just as are his two automobiles, his Caribbean condominium, and his mistress, the Corporate Assistant of Personal Affairs. Unfortunately, there is just no way to deduct legitimately a wife and seven children as a corporate expense. Suddenly, he must be legitimate when dealing with family. His million-dollar corporation shows a net profit of $12,000 a year, so it is with a great deal of indignation and self-righteousness that the corporate philanderer defends his position; he can't understand why an intelligent judge can't use this net figure to determine alimony and child support. Of course, out of the $12,000, the tycoon needs about $8,000 for his own basic, necessary living expenses and argues that his wife and children should be satisfied with $65 a week. His veiled threat is that any alimony award above $100 a week will force him to close his million-dollar business and go on welfare. In such an exaggerated but not so untypical case, most judges will not fall for the argument. Yet, to some degree, the husband is in the best position for he has the bargaining power, and he knows how to use it. Without the right lawyer, the wife's situation could be very serious.

Many husbands go to extreme lengths to avoid alimony.

CHET AND SARAH GOLDWIGG

Chet Goldwigg achieved the American dream. Continual hard work, day and night, seven days a week, paid off. He single-handedly built his computer business to an annual gross of $4,000,000. His family paid a high price for this success. Though they shared in his prosperity, they did not share much of his time. However, it was a lifestyle to which they accustomed themselves. His five children grew up without him at their football games, ballet recitals, and parent-teacher conferences. Home responsibility was left entirely to his dutiful wife, Sarah. She was the perfect wife for Chet—uncomplaining, subservient, and adoring. Raised in poverty, Sarah valued economic security above all else, and Chet filled that need well. Never wanting in material things, Sarah always indulged herself with the latest fashions, the most current hairdressers and decorators, and the best clubs. Chet also kept Sarah on his corporate payroll and took advantage of every possible tax break, which included deducting her cars, trips, and clothes. Many of his deductions were questionable, but the tax authorities never picked them up, buried as they were in the maze of his complex financial transactions. Sarah's financial serenity came suddenly to an end, however, when Chet was enticed by Barbara, a shrewd young woman who quickly worked her way up the corporate ladder from assistant bookkeeper to Chet's personal secretary.

Chet soon found himself in a bind. Originally, he had no intention of shedding his comfortable marital life and he was certainly unaware of Barbara's devious schemes designed to slowly but surely awaken Sarah to the truth. With each of Barbara's phone calls to her husband, Sarah could detect obvious inflections and double meanings which aroused suspicions. From then on, it was but a matter of time before Sarah pieced everything together. She soon questioned Chet's increasing number of business trips which seemed always to require Barbara's presence. Sarah was no fool. She was tolerant of Chet's lack of attention to her and the children, but she could not abide her husband sleeping with another woman. Therefore, Sarah decided matter-of-factly that she didn't need Chet as her husband. She had no doubt that she and the children could easily exist without his physical presence—they had done so for years—so she immediately filed for divorce. It never entered her mind that she would be jeopardizing her economic lifestyle or standard of living.

At first it wasn't easy for Sarah to find a lawyer. Not only did Chet have all the money, he also had a lot of friends and contacts in the business and professional world. She knew several lawyers but all of them were close friends of her husband. Without having anyone she could seek advice from, Sarah finally settled on one of the more reputable and respected lawyers in the community. Bradley Kingsley was known for his impeccable integrity and sense of ethics. Little did Sarah realize that these would not help her win her case. Bradley would have represented her well in an age of chivalry, but not in a bitter divorce contest. Matrimonials were not his forte. In fact, he took the case only because he knew most of the lawyers were not willing to go up against Sarah's husband, who was one of the leading figures in their city's financial circles. Bradley's sense of ethics dictated his accepting her case even though he was out of his field and, as he soon discovered, out of his league. From the beginning, every effort to seek disclosure of Chet's assets and income were met with stonewalls, delays, and adjournments. A rash of legal motions and procedural technicalities dragged each step in the lawsuit into a long, costly, and tiring battle. Sarah's discouragement and frustrations were matched by her attorney's sense of failure and disgust. Whenever Bradley succeeded in uncovering one corporate asset, he would find out that the asset had been transferred into the name of someone else. Or he would find that the asset was tied up as security on a large loan, which in turn was poured back into the business and could not be traced. New lawsuits had to be commenced to allege that these different transfers were a sham designed to defraud Chet's family of their rightful share of his wealth. Nor did the laws of the state help Sarah's cause. Chet and Sarah were not living in a community property state, and so the laws favored the spouse who had ownership of the assets. As in most marriages, everything was in Chet's name, including their $350,000 home. Title to property had always been the last thing on Sarah's mind as she tended to the needs of her family. Now she was in a state of shock as the realization sank in: After twenty-one years of marriage she owned nothing. And even more appalling, that was how the law viewed her situation, too. It became clear to Sarah that possession was not nine-tenths of the law—it was ten-tenths. The conflict finally became a dispute over how much money Chet was going to pay Sarah and the children to live on.

Chet's battery of lawyers made it clear that his present income was the key factor in determining alimony and child support. Overnight his computer firm suffered severe and somewhat inexplicable setbacks. Months before the case was scheduled for trial, Chet lost his largest customer, which accounted for one third of his firm's profits. This loss did not disturb Chet because he had arranged it! This good customer and close friend agreed to stop all purchases until the divorce was settled. Chet also utilized other available tax devices to increase his expenses, decrease his net earnings, and lower the economic growth of his company. When the case finally got to court, Chet's eloquent lawyer painted the sad picture of a once strong and independent entrepreneur—a man of business verve who achieved an American dream—who was now being destroyed by a bitter and greedy wife. He depicted Sarah as wanting to continue to live with a steady supply of furs and jewelry, while Chet was struggling to hold onto his quickly failing business. Ironically, Chet's lawyer showed the judge that the real cause of his economic loss was Sarah's irrational and destructive behavior, which not only interfered with poor Chet's thinking ability, but even worse, destroyed the children's love for their father. Chet's lawyer pulled out the old brainwashing accusation, claiming the five children's strong support for their mother was due to her brainwashing them into seeing their father as an evil, despicable man. In actuality, Sarah never resorted to this destructive behavior nor was it necessary. Her five children were mature enough to see the truth of the situation—their father *was* an evil, despicable man. Sarah's lawyer did counterattack nobly but feebly as he tried to paint the picture of a spurned and abandoned wife. However, he was able to evoke little sympathy for his well-dressed, jewel-bedecked client who was still strikingly beautiful at age 44.

As for the other woman, Barbara, that issue evaporated. Not only did Chet's lawyer indignantly deny any adultery, but he also righteously noted that this purely platonic and business relationship was sullied by a paranoid wife who made groundless accusations which finally broke up the marriage. Unfortunately, Sarah's lawyer had no proof of adultery even though he hired the best detective agency the day Sarah retained him. Chet was no patsy. When Sarah began inquiring about lawyers, word got back to Chet within hours. Chet knew his only vulnerable spot was his mistress and took immediate action. Chet promoted Barbara to an executive position at $38,000 a year. Unfortunately for their relationship, this attractive position was in Chet's West Coast office. The ever-ambitious Barbara quickly chose this high-paying promotion. (Unbeknownst to her corporate sugar daddy, her real love was Randy, the stockboy in computer construction, and she had Randy assigned to the Coast as soon as she got there!) Nor would she ever testify against Chet, knowing full well the cost of such an action. What she didn't know was that as soon as Chet's divorce was made final she and Randy would be unceremoniously and instantly dumped into the ranks of the unemployed.

At the end of the contested trial, the judge reserved decision. After one month of deliberations, he rendered a decision which reflected his doubts about everything he heard. In essence, he took all of the proof he heard on both sides with a grain of judicial salt and reached a result which placed him somewhere in the middle of all of the contentions. The judge found it hard to believe Chet's big business took such a sudden plunge without Chet's calculated desire to lessen alimony and child support. Yet, being a good judge, he couldn't base his decision on speculation and conjecture. He also doubted Chet's fidelity, but once again his sense of innate fairness would not let him assume that where there's suspicion, there may well be cheating. On the other hand, in case there was truth to Sarah's accusations, he felt compelled to give her and the children more than he might have. Before all of this marital trouble arose, Chet had been making $120,000 a year. By the time the divorce action came to trial, his income was $60,000 a year. The judge set Sarah's alimony at $18,000 a year and the children's support at $20,000 a year. Chet feigned great anger at a judge who could take $38,000 out of his $60,000 net income. He spent the next years rejoicing in the telling of his sad plight at the hands of a judicial system which took almost two-thirds of his income to support his wife and children. In fact, he was secretly overjoyed at the result. He didn't share this joy with his lawyers whom he blamed for the "horrible" result. Chet was too smart to tell even his own lawyers about the financial she-nanigans, which lowered his income.

The five children were grown and no longer eligible for support within seven years after the divorce. Chet's only remaining obligation was to pay Sarah her annual alimony of $18,000 a year. Not really a grand sum, considering that she had to pay taxes on the alimony, which left her about $14,000 a year. True, she was young and could get a job; in fact, Sarah did just that without much trouble. But she never considered the result of her action fair, as she watched Chet gain all of his business back within two years of the divorce and observed the kind of lifestyle he was leading with his new wife, the daughter of one of their closest friends. She never did find out that Chet's annual net income jumped to $90,-000 one year after the divorce, $120,000 two years later, and $180,000 the year after the last of his children became emancipated. So after twenty-one years of marriage, during which time Chet built up a business and Sarah raised the family, the economic division broke down to 90 percent for the husband and 10 percent for the wife.

What can you do if you are married to someone like Chet?

HOW TO FIND THE ASSETS

The key to finding the assets of a deceptive spouse is persistence. If you continually search and harass him with legal discovery motions to uncover his assets, he will finally realize that he just can't get away from his financial obligations. More important, he'll want to get his wife off his back! For example, when a spouse is hiding or transferring assets away to avoid alimony, there are some harsh remedies available under the law. Sequestration is a rarely used but effective legal tool which in many states allows a dependent spouse to seize the property of her mate and use it for family support. Many types of property are subject to sequestration, and the job of the sequestrator is to seize the property and dispose of it in any way the court directs. Sometimes this remedy is the only one available to protect a spouse from being financially deserted.

Many husbands flee home and state to avoid paying support or alimony. They pack all their money and personal property into the car. If possible, many would load up the real estate, too. Since this is not feasible, they try to sell their land before sneaking off, but time doesn't always permit this. A wife can have her lawyer immediately start an action for sequestration to protect her rights.

Another remedy, similar to sequestration, is called attachment. Not all states allow use of attachments in matrimonial actions. For example, in New York State, an order of attachment may be granted in any action *except* a matrimonial action. Attachment is a drastic measure which allows a spouse to go to court and get an order to hold the other spouse's property as security for the payment of any alimony. A bond is always required, and the party asking for this relief must convince the court that enforcement of any judgment would be totally frustrated without the order of attachment. These kinds of proceedings give a spouse a legal device which enables him or her to seize and hold onto his or her mate's property, in order to secure any alimony owed or which may become due and owing. Such proceedings are lengthy and complicated, and lawyers are often reluctant to utilize them except as a last resort. Many attorneys hesitate to use such extreme measures because they honestly believe that they can work out the alimony dispute without taking such cost and time. The problem with this approach is that when the lawyer finally discovers that he is dealing with an impossible spouse, it may be too late to find any property.

Perhaps the best way to defeat such a difficult spouse is to let him defeat himself. While it is true a husband trying to avoid alimony can resort to numerous ploys to throw investigators off his financial track, every step he takes to avoid alimony also has the effect of tying him up to some degree. If he has to hide an asset, he can't use it too easily. If he has to place an asset in someone else's name, then obviously he doesn't own the asset and runs the risks that go with that tactic. If he has to cut down on his earnings, shift business, finagle with the books, or toy with statistics, then he has to live with that precarious financial situation until the marital battle is over. And the longer the war continues, the harder it will be for him to maintain a façade of poverty. With a persistent wife, the husband may finally see the light—that the legal maneuvering will never cease until his real worth is discovered. He will then have to come to the bargaining table to try tŏ work out a fair and reasonable alimony settlement. Again, this result depends on the ability and perseverance of the woman's attorney. If a husband understands he's not going to get his wife off his back until the truth is discovered, he must capitulate. Why?

Firstly, he will want to resume normal financial activity which is impossible under a strained and tense situation where much of his worth is tied up or hidden. Besides peace of mind, he will also want to settle the case for fear of the tax collector. Any husband who goes

127

to the trouble of hiding assets and struggling to avoid alimony payments is often the same man who has made the effort through the years to avoid his tax responsibilities. The one fear hanging over him during the marital dispute is that full disclosure of his true assets—perhaps at a trial on the alimony issue—might reveal a history of tax evasion. He may finally meet his wife's demands just to keep his financial books from closer scrutiny.

Once the husband decides to negotiate alimony in good faith, there are countless ways to achieve a mutually satisfactory result. The usual request for alimony is for either a weekly support payment or one substantial lump sum payment. But there is no reason alimony can't be awarded in other forms, such as mortgage payments, life insurance policies, health insurance coverage, or other benefits.

For example, a Maine judge awarded a wife alimony by requiring the husband to make monthly mortgage payments on certain property, to maintain life insurance with his former wife as irrevocable beneficiary, and to obtain health insurance for her on his policy at his place of employment.[31] The Maine court specifically declared that the term "alimony" is not limited to direct money payments to a spouse. The court said that there is broad discretion in ordering alimony and stated, "Alimony must be reasonable both in amount and in the method of payment, giving regard to the situation, both at present and for the foreseeable future, of both spouses."

Turning over property in lieu of payments is another method of dealing with the alimony issue. A car or boat, the house or some other valuable asset can be substituted. It amounts to a form of lump sum alimony payment.

Few spouses are willing to pay an amount the receiving spouse thinks he or she deserves. And some go to great lengths to avoid it. Some of the more standard methods used to avoid alimony are:

1. Quitting a job.
2. Dropping all income-producing sources.
3. Transferring assets into someone else's name.
4. Hiding assets.
5. Moving away.
6. Remarrying and having children as quickly as possible.
7. Bringing aged parents into the house to care for them.
8. Refusing to pay alimony.
9. Paying bit by bit, but never the full amount, and never on time.
10. Introducing the ex-spouse to the perfect mate.

Chapter 13
THE ALIMONY BATTLE AFTER DIVORCE

The long struggle is over, and finally an alimony figure is agreed upon or ordered by the court. What happens if the receiving spouse can't exist on it or the paying spouse can't meet the weekly payments? Life after divorce is not always free of legal maneuvers. Post-divorce matrimonial issues frequently end up back in court.

To begin with, many disputes arise out of legitimate differences as to how much alimony has already been paid. Quite often a husband's record of payments does not match the wife's receipts of such payments. For some reason, the wife's accounts almost always reflect a lower amount than the husband believes he's paid. The judge is then left with the job of trying to sort out what she really did receive. The husband might claim he sent the checks in the mail or dropped off cash at the door. She'll say, "Not so." The ideal way to keep track of payments is through Family Court itself. In this way, the court will do all the record-keeping for you. Whatever system is used, it is important to itemize every payment you make or receive—in case future differences arise.

MISSING IN ACTION: HOW TO COLLECT DELINQUENT ALIMONY PAYMENTS

Sometimes an award of alimony is so unreasonably large that it causes the loser to quit his job, flee the jurisdiction, or take some other drastic action, so he will not have to pay any of it. Many wives walk out of the courtroom holding an alimony judgment, but that court paper won't buy the groceries or clothes. And if the husband and the money are gone, hers was a Pyrrhic victory.

JACK AND SALLY

After twenty-four years of marriage, it wasn't easy for Jack to face Sally and ask for a divorce. They had raised four children, shared the pain of a stillbirth, and suffered through economic hard times. They had weathered childhood diseases, broken arms, music lessons, Little League, and high school graduations. They had enjoyed vacations together in the Caribbean, with and without the children, drives to Disney World, weekend trips to the ocean, and now Jack had to tell Sally that he no longer loved her. He thought it best to leave out the part about Pam, the young receptionist at the Racquet Club. She was the reason Jack's three-times-a-week lunch-hour workouts expanded to five.

Jack's trim body and healthy good looks belied his emotional well-being. Much as he tried to rationalize, he was plagued with guilt. He knew he was being rotten. Because of this, he willingly consented to a most attractive separation agreement for Sally, including substantial alimony payments for the rest of her life. Liberated as she thought she was, she readily accepted the generous financial terms for several reasons. First, she felt the money was due her, since she had expected Jack to live with her for the remainder of their lives and share the financial fruits of their years of struggle. Now that she was losing Jack, there was no reason for her to lose the comfortable life that she expected to share with him. She'd make the best of being alone, but if she couldn't have Jack, she at least wanted his—or their—money. Second, since Jack wanted so badly to end the marriage, why shouldn't he pay a price for it? Third, there was no reason to let him have too much money to spend on Pam.

After the divorce, Jack thoroughly enjoyed his new life with Pam and, as time went by, his feelings of guilt lessened until, finally, he detested making out a large alimony check each week to a woman he no longer lived with and certainly no longer loved. Pam was a good sport about the situation, but in her own sly way, she made little digs that got under Jack's skin. For example, "Sally's a big girl now. Why can't she get a job like any other healthy red-blooded American woman?" or, "It's too bad we can't buy a Mercedes; you'd look so great behind the wheel, Jack. Can't we cut out an expense somewhere in our tight budget?" Slowly, Jack came to feel there was no reason for him to pay alimony.

Jack's attorney told him it might be difficult

to break the agreement but suggested the best approach would be to stop making payments altogether. When the payments stopped, Sally's protests put them back into court. She made the mistake of selecting a bad lawyer who let Jack's lawyer obtain adjournment after adjournment. Finally, Sally got a new lawyer to handle the appeal. By then she had run out of money, patience, and respect for the legal system. The lawyers drafted a new agreement which Sally decided to accept, just to end the frustrating and fruitless experience. For one year she would receive half the original amount agreed to, and the amounts would decrease annually until, after 10 years, she would receive nothing. Sally was left with a deep resentment for a legal system that favored the side which had the most money to spend on litigation, which permitted extensive delays, and which apparently refused to enforce agreements that were made in good faith by two competent and intelligent adults.

Unfortunately, Sally's experience is not uncommon, although the result of her case is not necessarily inescapable. A good attorney can more often than not persevere and enforce an ex-wife's alimony agreement.

Sometimes post-divorce alimony fights are part of a spouse's game plan. For instance, one way to end a bitter marital alimony battle is to simply give in to all demands, even if they are unreasonable. Most ethical people find this difficult to do, but there is always a special breed of person who finds it easy to say anything to please the listener and then goes ahead and does what he or she wants. Such a husband could easily sign an agreement promising his wife substantial alimony, knowing full well that he will never pay it. His only concern is the short run—getting out of his marriage. He'll give her anything she asks for so that he gets his divorce. He's in a big rush to marry his girlfriend and doesn't want to spend two years battling in court over alimony. So, if he takes home $185 a week and his wife wants $110 alimony, he instructs his lawyer to draw the papers and give her what she wants. He signs the agreement, the divorce is put through, and he gets remarried. Three weeks later his ex-wife calls her lawyer to say she received a check for only $50 or, worse yet, nothing at all. Her lawyer files a petition in court to enforce terms of the separation agreement, and when the case finally comes up months later, the husband's lawyer explains to the judge there's no way his client can pay $110 weekly out of earnings of $185. Besides that, his client has remarried, and they expect a child. Of course, the judge can take the hard line and say, "You agreed to it, buddy, and you can't back out now." If the court takes this hard line, the judge may eventually threaten the husband with jail. Adjustments will eventually be made, and the husband's agreement to pay alimony wasn't worth the paper it was written on. You wonder why his ex-wife wasn't more suspicious at the time of the divorce. But once a cad, always a cad; he probably enticed her into marriage with promises he never kept.

Sometimes it is the judge who may be the cause of endless alimony litigation after divorce. A court's unreasonable judgment dampens the chances for enforcing his own order. After hearing a case, a judge renders his decision, based on the facts presented to him. He may entirely miss the mark, leaving both lawyers quite distraught. The first problem is that the facts presented to him may not be true. Equally difficult is that he makes his judgment on how he views the facts, and his perspective may be off base because of his own personal failings, inability, or prejudice. However, most times the verdict does fall within a broad range of reasonableness with which both sides can live.

LOWERING THE AWARD

A reasonable alimony award at one point in time may become unreasonable as time passes. A highly placed executive agrees to pay his wife substantial alimony, and then he loses his job. A man with a good income is disabled through accident or sickness, and his new income is meager. In these and similar situations, there may be no way for an alimony award to be met. But that doesn't allow the husband to unilaterally reduce his payments or stop them. Many a husband who assumed he could stop paying alimony because he was laid off or sick was later surprised by an unsympathetic judge who told him only a court can change an existing court order—and ordered him to make up the back payments.

Nor can you simply escape an alimony obligation by moving to another state. Many states have passed a Uniform Reciprocal Enforcement of Support Law which allows proceedings to enforce alimony orders in other states. If your husband leaves Pennsylvania and moves to Alabama, you don't have to run down to Alabama after him. You go to your local Family Court and file a petition under the Uniform Law. Your local Family Court will contact the Alabama Family Court nearest to where your spouse lives, and he will be brought into that local court to answer your petition. There are some obvious disadvantages to such long-distance court proceedings. If you can't afford to travel to Alabama to personally give your side of the story, your ex-husband may have the advantage of a more persuasive first-hand appearance. A local counsel or public attorney may be assigned to represent your interest, but there is sometimes a natural, subconscious inclination to give more credence to someone standing before you.

If you want to change a court order, you have to go back to court to do it. Your attorney makes a motion to modify the existing alimony award due to a change in circumstances. The burden of proof is always on the one seeking the change. Therefore, you have to demonstrate a significant change in financial circumstances since the time of the original order.

Obviously, the law does not countenance people going back and forth into court to see if they can do better with a different judge. The idea of allowing one to go into court to seek modification of an alimony order is not to reargue the case but to seek change based on new and substantially different circumstances.

INCREASING THE AWARD

Just as changed circumstances could warrant the lowering of an alimony award, so too they can justify an increase. Somehow this is harder to do. If a wife wins a substantial alimony award, and later her husband finds it impossible to meet such a commitment, there is little alternative for a court but to lower the award. However, when a wife gets modest alimony, and then comes back for more, courts are often less sympathetic.

Let's take a typical case where a wife would feel justified in seeking greater alimony.

BETSY AND WALT

At the time of their divorce, Walt was a neophyte stockbroker with low earnings. His wife, Betsy, agreed to accept $50 a week alimony out of his net earnings of $14,000 a year. In the next three years, Walt's income soared to $60,000 a year. Betsy went back to court and asked for much higher alimony based on his higher earnings. It seemed logical to Betsy that she should share in his good fortune; she also knew that if Walt struck out as a stockbroker and joined the ranks of the unemployed, she would lose her alimony. But the court ruled an emphatic "No." The judge said their marriage was over, and there was no reason Betsy should be entitled to "continually link her economic fortunes to his." The court reasoned that Walt had never provided a high standard of living for Betsy when they were husband and wife, and her award of $50 a week was properly based on the economic realities of their marriage.

While an award of alimony can be modified after divorce, this legal right usually works more to the advantage of the spouse seeking to lower the alimony.

REMARRIAGE AND ALIMONY

Many husbands have added problems meeting support obligations if they remarry. While the ex-wife's remarriage stops her alimony payments, his remarriage has no effect on his duty to support. And with the great upsurge of remarriage, more and more step-families find the economic going very difficult. It's not unusual for the husband to go back to court to plead for lower alimony because his new family responsibilities are draining his wallet.

With this rising incidence of divorce and remarriage, courts are often faced with balancing the needs of first, second, and sometimes third families. When the divorce is granted in marriage No. 1, it might be easy for everyone to agree that the wife and two children should get $65 weekly out of husband's $120 paycheck. Complications arise when the husband remarries and has two more children. He finds it difficult to support both families and in time falls behind in his support payments to family No. 1. His ex-wife goes to Family Court to get alimony and child support arrears, but now the husband appears the one deserving sympathy—a man struggling to take care of two families. He rightfully points out that his income of $120 a week is a small pie and leaves it to the judge to divide it up any way that appears fair. In reality, any fair division can now no longer give $65 a week to family No. 1 and leave only $55 a week for family No. 2. And it shouldn't be forgotten that the husband himself must eat and be clothed.

Wife No. 1's point of view is clear: Why should she and her children suffer because her irresponsible husband voluntarily took on a new family, one he could not afford? Her point is valid and one recognized by the law. Courts generally hold that family No. 1 gets top priority in this kind of situation. While a court cannot punish the husband's second family and deny them the right to exist, in balancing the finances the court will give greater weight to the first family.

It's becoming common to see even third or fourth remarriages, which further aggravate the financial plight of the busy husband. Such a man doesn't even need a lawyer; he just appears in court on one side with all of his ex-wives on the other, turns to the judge and says, "I'll do whatever you want, Your Honor. I still make $120 a week, so you can divide up my 'pie' any way you want,

138

and I'll live by your order." By then, his former wives have little interest in his 'pie." At that point, his ex-wives all agree on one thing: Better he should be jailed than marry again!

While an alimony-paying husband's remarriage often makes matters worse for him, his wife's remarriage is a blessing to him. Everyone knows that alimony is supposed to cease as soon as the spouse receiving the payments gets married. That's the easy case.

The hard case arises when the ex-wife enjoys her alimony payments as much as she enjoys her new boyfriend. She decides it makes absolutely no sense to remarry and lose her meal ticket. Why can't she have her cake and eat it too? In today's open society, living together is no longer unusual, nor does it carry the stigma it once did. Yet, the law is still not ready to accommodate this lifestyle. New York law, for example, holds that an ex-wife is still entitled to receive her alimony even if she has a live-in boyfriend—with one condition: That they do not hold themselves out to the community as man and wife. As recently as 1978, New York's highest court held that where a man and woman clearly maintained an unmarried status, and made this clear to the outside world by keeping separate names on their mailbox and by other acts, the woman was still entitled to receive alimony from her ex-spouse.[32] However, Judge Sol Wachtler noted in a dissent opinion that the court's decision "leaves the courts powerless to relieve the former husband of the obligation of subsidizing his former wife's affairs no matter how unfair this may be under the circumstances."

Needless to say, an ex-spouse does not enjoy paying his hard-earned money to a live-in couple. Legislation has been introduced in New York to prevent this kind of situation, but until the law changes, an ex-husband must keep the alimony flowing even if his ex-wife is using it to buy jeans and liquor for her new boyfriend. "Justice" often renders strange results!

One way to avoid state law which provides that a spouse can receive alimony even if he or she lives with another is to specifically provide in a separation agreement that alimony will cease upon remarriage or when the spouse receiving alimony cohabits with another. For instance, a recent New York case upheld a separation agreement which stated that the husband would pay alimony to the wife

> Until the death of the husband, the death of the wife or the remarriage of the wife. The term 're-marriage' as used herein shall include not only ceremonial marriage, but also the same set of circumstances as would result in the wife being a partner with an unrelated male adult in a single domestic unit.[33]

The New York court found this contract term valid and held that the wife was bound by the clear language of the agreement and therefore lost her right to alimony as soon as she formed a live-in liaison with a man after her divorce. The court further held that her right to alimony could not be revived when this affair later broke up. The ex-wife's right to alimony was extinguished under the agreement and could not be revived.

In another New York case, a separation agreement provided the wife was entitled to alimony payments which would terminate upon her death or remarriage or if the wife lived with someone else before the divorce became final. Cohabiting was defined in this agreement as the "regular living together with a man for a period exceeding six months." The New York courts upheld the validity of this clause and terminated the wife's right to alimony, since it was established that she had cohabited as defined in the agreement.[34]

ENFORCEMENT OF COURT ORDERS

If an ex-spouse has been ordered to pay alimony, he can be later held in contempt and jailed or fined if he fails to obey the court order without good cause. Yes, husbands still go to jail for not paying alimony. But they don't get put away because they can't afford to support their wives; they are locked up because they flagrantly disobeyed a court order. So if a husband makes $250 a week, signs a separation agreement which gives his wife $40 a week alimony, and fails to meet this obligation, his wife may take him back to court. After a full hearing, the judge may issue a court order directing him to pay the $40 a week along with back alimony owed. If the husband continues to ignore the court order, the next time he's hauled back into court, the judge may issue a stern warning that next time he's back in court he'll go to jail. If the order still is ignored, the judge may issue a warrant for the man's arrest. He will be put in jail not so much because he didn't pay her the money, but because his contemptuous behavior shows that he will not obey the law as clearly spelled out by the judge. Before the judge sends him to jail, he makes sure that the husband was in willful contempt of the court order, and that he really could make the payments but refused to do so. The wife just wants her money; if the husband reluctantly offers it as the deputy sheriff is escorting him from the courtroom, the judge will almost always allow this payment to purge the husband of his contempt, thus setting him free.

    If the husband can show that he did not intentionally avoid making the payments—for instance, he was financially unable to make payments—then the court might not hold him in contempt. However, he will still be responsible to pay the back alimony as soon as he is able. He can't escape this responsibility. And alimony, like child support, is a debt which cannot be discharged in bankruptcy. In other words, if an ex-husband goes broke, he can file for bankruptcy and wipe out all of his bills, but he will still be liable to pay any back alimony still owed. Many ex-husbands find themselves overwhelmed by alimony arrears that they let get out of hand over the years. When an ex-husband misses one payment here and one payment there, as the years pass he may suddenly discover he owes his ex-wife thousands of dollars. Sooner or later the day of reckoning comes, and he will most likely be paying arrearages long after his actual support obligation has ceased. For example, if his wife remarries, he will no longer have to make alimony payments—but if he owes her $3,500 in back alimony, he will have to pay off this debt.

Once back alimony starts to build up, the distraught ex-wife has several ways to get her money. One extreme remedy is to go to court and obtain a judgment garnisheeing the husband's wages. It is prepared by her lawyer and delivered to the sheriff, who then serves it on the spouse's employer. Many states have a limit to the percentage of the spouse's wages that can be taken each week through a garnishment, but since such a limitation is usually designed to preserve the debtor's family, courts don't usually limit the percentage when the debt sought is for the family itself in the form of child support or alimony.

Sometimes a Family Court can strongly urge a spouse to agree to give part of his wages each week toward paying up the support or alimony he owes. This court urging can amount to a not so subtle coercion: The husband's choice is to agree to the court's suggestion or go to jail for past failure to make support payments. Instead of a garnishment, this is called a wage assignment and is "voluntarily" consented to by the husband to allow his employer to deduct the money from his paycheck and send it directly to the court.

There are other legal remedies available to the ex-wife seeking collection of back alimony, but realistically speaking, they all usually involve lengthy and costly litigation. The battle seems endless, and worse, fruitless. That is why most lawyers would prefer one final lump sum alimony settlement rather than small weekly payments and their potential to cause ongoing battle. An attorney might advise his client to accept a $20,000 lump sum figure, rather than $50 a week alimony. Even if she is 50 years old and has a life expectancy of 24 years, which would mean anticipated alimony of about $60,000 over the years, it might be wiser for her to grab the $20,000 and run. Why is this preferable? First, the husband could drop dead after the first $50 payment, and she would get no more. Or she could remarry shortly after the divorce or die. Or, he could find it difficult to pay—or make it difficult to collect. Whatever the reason, weekly alimony is problematical and has left many ex-wives bitter and broke.

SURVIVAL WITHOUT ALIMONY

You lost your battle. It isn't fair, but so what else is new? Life is full of bad breaks, injustices, and raw deals, but there's nothing you can do but roll with the punch and live without alimony. In other words, you'll have to make it on your own—and you will. Looking back on your marriage, it should be clear that any person who can survive a tough marriage, possibly raising children and taking care of the household, certainly has the ability to succeed.

To put your ability to work, you'll have to pull yourself together and take the following steps:

1) Take stock of yourself. Assess your own abilities and capabilities to see what role in life will bring you satisfaction and sufficient income. You may have to look all the way back to your premarriage days when you enjoyed a particular course in school or had a job that interested you. Or you may just have to look back a few years to see what activities you were involved with. You'll also have to consider seeking additional education or skills in a particular field.

2) You should begin beating a path to all of your friends and family to discuss your future prospects. Over the years, these people may have viewed you as a dependent housewife and parent, and it's time that they look at you as an independent individual, perhaps one who needs their help to get into the working world. An exchange of ideas, coupled with their contacts, may present new opportunities to you.

3) Prepare a resumé and begin circulating it to the appropriate businesses, industries, and government in your community—places where you would like to work. Keep them circulating and up-to-date so that yours is not shoved into a file of forgotten resumés. Don't forget to state on your resumé your success in raising a family and your full-time availability if your children are grown. You'd be surprised how many employers prefer to hire a mature, stable woman who has gained experience and insights, as opposed to a young person fresh out of school. You are considered a good risk as you will probably stay with your employer for years, and you probably won't

need maternity leave. Even at age 50 or 55, you can offer an employer ten to twenty years of loyal service, and that's usually a lot more than a company expects out of a 20-year-old.

4) If, following your divorce, you feel trapped in your spouse's domain surrounded by former friends, restaurants and lifestyle, there's nothing wrong with starting a new life in a different community. Perhaps you should consider an area with good job prospects for a person in your position and an area with a climate that suits your taste. Obviously, you shouldn't automatically move away if you have your own friends and family in your home area. While leaving can be construed as running away and is not usually the best answer to anyone's problems, it should not be ruled out.

5) If you really believe you can't make it, don't hesitate to see a psychiatrist or psychologist. There is no shame in seeking help, and many people in today's society, at some time in their lives, seek such help. "Temporary insanity" may be the result of a marital breakup. It's at this point that many spouses have the greatest need of professional help. More than one distraught spouse on the verge of suicide has been made to recognize his or her own worth as a human being.

If one of your problems is no alimony or child support, you can always go on welfare as a last resort. Ironically, this is the best way to reverse the judge who gave you no alimony. As soon as you begin to receive public assistance, governmental authorities will start looking for your ex-spouse very quickly. Every state has a public policy which strongly opposes the taxpayers' supporting any family member when another may be able to do it. Someone else in the family is always sought to pay first. This rule includes ex-spouses, too, and as soon as you start receiving welfare, the court will look to that person for support until you are able to make it on your own without public assistance.

Your problems aren't necessarily over when you get divorced. Enforcing the alimony order, modifying it, collecting arrears, remarriage, losing your right to alimony, and living without it are all realities. Alimony after divorce can be a continuing source of conflict, but even the post-divorce conflict serves one healthy purpose: It is a constant reminder to the ex-spouses that their decision to divorce was the right one!

Chapter 14
THE TAX MAN COMETH ALWAYS

Not even the sacredness of marriage and the tragedy of divorce are immune from the tax collector. Substantial tax consequences flow from any change in marital status. Alimony, child support, and other aspects of separation agreements have specific effects with regard to tax on a divorcing couple's economic situation. The federal tax officials are concerned about where a married couple's money is coming from and going to, and—most important—where it is. The government wants its share, after all.

When considering the tax consequences of your marital dispute, be acutely aware that good tax planning can make a real difference in negotiations, settlements, and the quality of life after divorce. Tax aspects of a settlement must be evaluated to understand the full significance of the agreement.

DAVID AND NICOLE

When David and Nicole parted after fourteen years of marriage, their only bone of contention was alimony. At the beginning, they decided there was no place for children in their future. Instead, they would devote their time to each other and to an exciting business venture they started while attending business school. They envisioned their computerized business form company as the road to quick wealth, but it turned into a long hard struggle which was producing a modest though comfortable living by the time their marital troubles began. They agreed to part amicably and did so after some hard negotiations over terminating their business partnership. It was finally agreed that Dave would keep the business, and Nicole would receive $90,000 from him in full settlement of all of their differences, both marital and business. Since Dave did not have that kind of money, it was stipulated that, starting one year after the signing of the agreement, he would pay Nicole $500 monthly for five years and then $1,000 monthly for the next five years. Both assumed the money would be treated as alimony so that David could deduct the payments, and Nicole would pay the tax.

Both they and their lawyers were unaware of a tax rule stating that periodic payments are considered alimony only if paid for at least ten years *and* in accord with the ten-percent rule. Under this rule, the periodic payment allowable as deductible alimony is limited to ten percent of the lump sum per year, in this case $9,000 or $750 a month. David and Nicole's agreement did not satisfy the ten-percent rule, since she would be receiving $1,000 monthly for the last five years. This unexpected tax result made a substantial difference in both of their incomes during the last five-year period, and David somewhat bitterly harbored the belief that Nicole and her lawyer had been aware of this tax ramification and had taken advantage of his ignorance.

ALIMONY

As a general rule, alimony is normally reportable for tax purposes as income by the spouse receiving it and as a deduction by the spouse paying it. Until a few years ago, alimony had been a "below the line" deduction; that is, it could only be claimed by those individuals who itemized deductions, which meant that if you didn't own a house with a mortgage, chances are you weren't able to claim alimony payments as an income tax deduction. Now, if the payment qualifies as deductible alimony, it can be deducted by an individual who takes a standard deduction.

To be tax deductible, alimony has to qualify under certain rules. First, the payments must be made pursuant to some form of decree or by agreement. Voluntary payments made prior to a court decree or before a separation agreement is made don't count to the tax collector. To be deductible, the payments cannot be made voluntarily; they must be required. For example, if a court order requires a husband to pay $50-a-week alimony to his ex-wife, and he pays her $70, the additional $20 *cannot* be deducted by the husband nor does the wife have to report it as income.

Another requirement for alimony to be deductible to the husband and includable in the wife's income is that the payments must be "periodic." To qualify as a periodic payment, there must be an indefiniteness about the payment. For example, it must be a fixed amount over an indefinite period (such as, "$50 a week until death or remarriage"), or an indefinite amount for a fixed or definite period (such as, "five percent of the husband's gross income for fifteen years").

Lump sum payments generally do not qualify as deductible alimony. However, under certain circumstances lump sum payments paid in installments can qualify as a tax deduction. So if the husband agrees to pay his wife a lump sum of $72,000 over a twelve-year period at a rate of $500 a month, the payments will be deductible. Payments of any lump sum made on an installment basis for a period of more than ten years are considered "periodic," and are viewed as deductible. This ten year period, by the way, is measured from the date of the decree or agreement. A word of caution: the Internal Revenue Service strictly adheres to the ten-year rule, and it must be *more* than ten years—not a day less. Yet, even this tax rule has an exception; lump sum installment payments of ten years or less can qualify as periodic payments if they are conditional. In other words, if the payment will terminate upon the happening of a contingency, it is considered a "periodic" payment and can be deducted. For example, if a spouse agrees to pay to his or her mate the sum of $100 a month for a term of eight years, it would not qualify as a periodic payment. But if the $100 a month was to be paid for eight years, or "terminated upon remarriage or death," the payment would be considered periodic and deductible. This is a so-called "contingent" payment. In the case above, the payment is contingent upon the wife surviving the full eight years and not remarrying. As such, it becomes deductible to the husband and includable in the wife's income. As a general rule, most alimony agreements provide for the termination of the payments upon remarriage and so would qualify as tax deductible item for husbands and as income to wives.

There are other types of payments that may also qualify as deductible alimony. For example, if a husband agrees to pay his wife's medical expenses or her mortgage payment, in certain cases such sums are considered periodic and therefore deductible. It should be clear that the tax aspects to marriage and divorce are not so clear.

Sometimes tax ramifications must outweigh the personal feelings which are so common to marital disputes. For example, many husbands are very much against alimony but are happy to pay child support. Yet, it is better for income tax purposes if the man's financial statement allocates a higher percentage of support payments to alimony since they will be deductible. The husband may say, "I won't pay that woman one cent of alimony," but he'll be cutting off his nose to spite his face. The rule, in fact, is that a periodic payment is always considered alimony unless specifically called "child support."

CHILD SUPPORT

Child support is *not* tax deductible. Nor is it considered income to the one who receives it. But payment of child support may enable the party paying it to claim the dependency exemption for his or her child. It is the general presumption that the parent who has custody is entitled to take this exemption. (The exemption until recently was $750, but has been raised to $1,000 per year.) However, there are circumstances in which the parent who doesn't have custody may qualify to take the exemption for the child.

If a separation agreement specifically provides that the noncustodial parent paying child support is entitled to the exemption, that parent may be able to get the exemption as long as payments are at least $600 per year per child. For example, if an agreement provides a husband must pay $15-a-week child support and that he is entitled to the dependency exemption for the child, he would qualify for the $1,000 annual deduction, since he would be paying child support of $780 annually. But without a specific clause in the agreement, he could not take the exemption.

Sometimes a noncustodial parent can take the exemption even when it's not provided in an agreement, but two tests must be met. First, he must pay $1,200 a year for each child for whom he claims an exemption. Second, he must withstand any claims by the custodial parent that he or she has provided more than $1,200 for the child's support. The presumption, however, is that the custodial parent is entitled to take the exemption.

IDA AND SHERMAN STANHAUER

Paul Rein was a shrewd and ingenious lawyer. He was always figuring the angles for his clients, and his imaginative thinking made even the simplest cases intricate. When Sherman Stanhauer came into his office for "an easy divorce," attorney Rein saw the potential for an exciting tax coup. Sherman and his wife, Ida, had already agreed to the financial terms to end their marriage. Sherman was going to pay Ida $400 a month to support her and their three children. Sherman merely wanted attorney Rein to draw up the agreement and get the divorce over with as quickly as possible. Rein did exactly what was asked of him, but he also managed to obtain for his client tax deductions of $6,000 a year!

It seemed incredible to Sherman that he could pay $400 a month for his family, or a total of $4,800 a year, and walk away with $6,000 worth of income tax deductions. And the explanation was really quite simple. Sherman's attorney drew a separation agreement for the couple which provided that Ida would receive $100-a-month alimony, $150-a-month child support, or a total of $1,800 a year for the three children, with a provision allowing Sherman to take three exemptions, and lastly, that Sherman would pay directly to the bank holding the home mortgage the sum of $150 a month as his liability for the interest and taxes on their house mortgage payment. Sherman did not understand this peculiar division of the $400 per month he was willing to pay for supporting his family, but he quickly saw the light when his attorney explained that the alimony payment was deductible and that amounted to $1,200 per year; that Sherman was entitled to take $3,000 of exemptions for the three children, since he was providing each of them with the minimum $600-a-year child support; and finally, that Sherman could take the monthly payment toward interest and taxes as a deduction, and that this amounted to $1,800 a year. Grand total: $6,000 worth of deductions and exemptions. Sherman was so elated he volunteered to give Ida an additional $100 a month alimony, which he could now afford because of his substantial deductions. Attorney Rein was pleased with his accomplishment too—and was astonished when Sherman neglected to pay his attorney fees. He finally did pay his bill, but only after discovering that a good part of this legal fee was also deductible as legal tax advice.

153

By utilizing the $600 rule in separation agreements, a husband can end up with more in deductions than he actually pays in child support. A good tax planning attorney can obtain for his client substantial tax savings from these kinds of tax rules.

OTHER TAX CONSIDERATIONS

There are many factors to consider when weighing the tax implications of your divorce. Take a look at the sale or transfer of marital property. A spouse who transfers his interest in the house to his wife as part of the divorce settlement may incur tax liability for the transfer. If a woman sells her half interest in the house, she may incur a capital gains tax on profit from the sale.

Another aspect of matrimonial actions which has tax consequences is legal fees. Legal fees are not a deductible item for defending or prosecuting a divorce or separation action. However, legal fees incurred for tax advice in a divorce or separation can be deductible. Likewise, a wife can deduct the portion of a legal fee she incurs pursuing collection of her alimony.

Another key aspect to marital tax planning relates to the *filing status* of the divorcing couple. With the end of the marriage the parties file as individuals. The custodial parent has the right to file as head of household so long as she is bearing most of the cost of maintaining the children even if she doesn't get the child support exemption. The noncustodial parent who pays child support and is taking the child support exemption generally cannot qualify to file as head of household. There are also intricate rules regarding separation situations. As a general rule, if the parties are separated pursuant to a separation agreement, they cannot file separately. They must file either "married, jointly," or "married, separately." Only in very limited circumstances can separated spouses file as "single." However, if they are separated pursuant to a court decree of separation, each can file as single.

Over the years, filing status has been an important consideration in marital cases. Traditionally, married couples received better tax breaks than single people. In a turnabout, the I.R.S. changed the tax advantages for filing. It is now often more advantageous to file as "single" rather than "married, separately" or "married, jointly." This policy has led a few couples to get divorced on December 31 and remarried on January 1. The key date for the determination of marital status for filing has always been the last day of the year. The I.R.S. has cracked down on this practice recently and is not allowing such couples to receive the benefits of single filing status.

Another potential area for disagreement is division of the tax refund. It's not unusual for a married couple to get some money back each year upon filing their joint return; when their marriage comes to an end, they may still be awaiting their refund check. The most common solution is to divide the refund equally, but if the couple is fighting over terms—such as who pays the wife's attorney—that expected refund check can be used as a bargaining tool to resolve other differences. For instance, the husband can agree that the wife will get the entire check in exchange for which she agrees to pay her own attorney fees. There are endless ways to handle every tax aspect of a divorce. What really matters is not precisely how each various tax matter is handled but that they are not overlooked.

Finally, consideration must always be given to how child support and alimony should be allocated. Savings can be immense for both sides by allowing the person in a higher bracket to take the tax benefits of deductions

155

for support or alimony. Unfortunately, a common mistake of many couples is to lump child support and alimony together. This unplanned approach can cause financial loss, sometimes to the wife, sometimes to the husband, sometimes to the children—but never to the tax collector.

A client should always ask his or her lawyer what the divorce settlement will mean taxwise. And the client should make sure he or she understands what the settlement will do for him in terms of dollars and cents in his pocket—both before and after taxes. Too often, the issue of taxes is swept under the rug by the attorneys, not out of ignorance but a well-intentioned desire to eliminate one source of conflict for the battling couple. When lawyers finally get their clients to agree on an amount of child support, alimony, or lump sum settlement after a long and protracted legal battle, they are in no mood to raise an issue for renewal of hostilities by discussing the intricate tax implications. Sometimes such an approach may be warranted where the emotional and psychological well-being of a spouse is in greater jeopardy than the person's financial well-being. But the tax factor *can* be significant.

Chapter 15
THE JUDGE

In a contested matrimonial dispute, the parties frequently find themselves in and out of court over different issues. It's not unusual for them to appear before a different judge every time. Different judges have different points of view, and the results of each proceeding may differ. A certain consistency is sometimes lost, and this can make the road of justice a perilous one. In fact, some lawyers spend endless time jockeying for the "right" judge to hear their case, at the expense of preparing for trial. They believe a case can be "won" or "lost" before the case is even heard, depending on the judge assigned.

No matter how they may be viewed, judges must be open-minded and listen only to the facts that are revealed on the witness stand. They are also allowed to observe the way the witness acts. Judges closely scrutinize each witness. The law in fact allows a trial judge to be influenced by the "demeanor" of a witness, and demeanor has a very broad meaning.

Ever aware that their case may rise or fall on how the client appears in court, many lawyers take pains to

157

dictate even the clothes their client wears when he or she enters the courtroom. They believe that their client's dress should reflect the kind of case presented. A woman who is crying poverty and financial neglect should not enter the courtroom in a fur coat. Instead she should wear a rather plain dress, no jewelry, little makeup; it may also help if her expression is a beseeching one. The attorney for the husband may want to paint the same picture—one of a man who can't afford much support because of his difficult economic situation. He should dress accordingly. On the other hand, there could be a case in which a woman client is to appear quite well off. If she is the wife of an extremely wealthy man and is seeking substantial alimony, she must convey a high standard of living, for the court will be asked to give her sufficient alimony so that she can continue to live as she is accustomed to doing. In that kind of case, she might well wear her finest jewelry, furs, and designer dress.

However judges handle their job, they remain the ultimate factor in a disputed matrimonial case. In the courtroom, their word is law. They bring into the courtroom their own background and beliefs. It is inevitable that their life experiences will bear upon their decisions. Perhaps for this reason, ninety percent of all marital differences are resolved between the couple, rather than leaving the matter to a stranger.

When a case can't be worked out and finally does end up in court, odds are that it will receive fair treatment. The judicial system is intentionally designed to give an individual judge broad discretion to work out equitable results in a matrimonial case. We still have not quite reached the "1984" era of computerized justice where battling parties feed facts into a machine to have it spit back a court decision. With all of their human frailties, judges usually meet the high challenge and responsibility of their office.

Chapter 16
TRENDS

While many states have been considering laws to update their traditional view of alimony, it was the United States Supreme Court decision in *Orr versus Orr* which gave the immediate impetus for revamping alimony provisions. One state which typifies such legislative activity is New York. It enacted a complete revision of their alimony provisions during its 1980 legislative session.

This new law encompasses the general principle of a more equitable distribution of real and personal property acquired during a marriage. The law attempts to prevent one spouse from being victimized financially because assets acquired during the marriage are all placed in the name of the other spouse. The law also makes alimony available to the husband as well as the wife and eliminates the punitive idea of withholding alimony because of marital fault. The law requires all marital property be divided equitably between the married parties, based on the circumstances of the case and of the respective parties. In determining the equitable disposition, the court considers factors, including income and property of each party at the time of marriage and at the time of the divorce; the length of the marriage; the age and physical and mental health of the parties; the loss of inheritance and pension rights when the marriage is dissolved; any existing temporary alimony; and either spouse's contribution toward acquisition of property in the other's name, including joint efforts or expenditures and contributions and services as a spouse, parent, wage-earner, and homemaker; and contributions to the career or career potential of the other party; probable future financial circumstances of each party; and any other factor which the court shall expressly find to be just and proper.

The new law also provides a lump sum award to fulfill one side's claim to a share in a business, corporation, or profession. The law allows a court to make any provision regarding use and occupancy of the marital home and its household effects. This law changes the New York law so property held in the name of one partner can be awarded to either or both spouses on an equitable basis.

The stated purpose of the law is to make provision for spousal maintenance, formerly known as alimony, to give the person needing support means to become self-sufficient. Proponents of the law say alimony too frequently caused dependence and was neither beneficial to the party paying support nor to the party receiving it. In one legislative memorandum to justify the legislation, it is stated that:

> Marriage in current times is, in fact, a partnership which is not fully recognized under the existing law. The partnership accumulates assets during the time of the marriage which most frequently results from both spouses' efforts, whether or not both are contributing financially to the

marriage. Present law gives the court no discretion to divide those assets in an equitable manner at the termination of the marriage. Presently, the court must award to each spouse all property held in their respective names. This is an extremely artificial and unfair means of reaching an equitable agreement at the termination of the marriage.

Although equitable distribution legislation is geared for remedying unjust and inequitable results which harm the woman in marriage, the National Organization for Women (NOW) opposes such proposals unless they specifically provide for a presumption of an equal division of property. NOW favors a law which states explicitly that all marital property is presumed to belong to both marriage partners equally, and that, when the marriage ends, all the property should be divided in half. NOW wants laws to presume that all marital property is equally owned, since marriage itself is an equal partnership.

The alimony law recently enacted in New York State implies that all marital property will be distributed equitably between the parties. As attractive as that may sound for a wife, NOW fears that such a law is a step backward for women. They contend that an equal distribution law without a fifty-fifty presumption will rarely result in a wife receiving her full half. Without a law which presumes equality, NOW fears the court will start to consider the marital property at zero percent for the wife and one-hundred percent for the husband and then adjust the amounts from there. Instead, NOW believes that a court should start at a fifty-fifty split and, if circumstances warrant, adjust from there.

There are several reasons NOW believes the woman will rarely receive her fair share without a presumption of equality. The organization contends women rarely

161

have a complete knowledge of the property owned and acquired during the marriage. The husband usually runs the business and controls the financial aspects of the marriage and therefore has the ability to conceal marital assets. Finally, since society, the bench, and the bar are still male oriented and male dominated, marital situations may continue to be viewed in the traditional chauvinistic sense, which considers the breadwinner as performing a more valuable economic role than the homemaker, NOW believes.

But no matter how alimony is defined and no matter what laws are passed in an attempt to provide equitable economic dealings between spouses, fairness will not result until attitudes change. New York can create the perfect equitable distribution statute, but it will not guarantee equitable results. Community property states themselves have discovered that there are many ways to get around the equal sharing concept of their laws. What will really abolish the historical concept of alimony and replace it with a fair division of the marital pie will be the changed mentality of society. It is clear the trend is toward considering marriage as a real partnership. Marriages may more and more encompass a true economic partnership and financial equality. Just as the husband who works in the outside business world and makes the money will be treated as an equal partner within the home (that is, joint custody), so too will the wife who spends all of her time working within the house be treated as an equal partner outside the home, in relation to her husband's work efforts. The fruits of the entire marital relationship, borne in the home as well as outside the home, will all be considered as belonging to both marriage partners. Traditional alimony has less significance in such a relationship. It is this new attitude which will eventually end alimony as we know it today. More and more states will follow the lead of Virginia, which considers "the monetary and the nonmonetary contribution of each party to the well-being of the family unit" a key factor in awarding permanent alimony.

However, while attitudes and values are changing, the law lags behind. But the gap is closing, and our fifty states' alimony laws have changed more radically in the past ten years than they had in the previous century. As respect for individual rights becomes as paramount within a marriage as it is outside the family unit, the alimony of today undoubtedly will be viewed with disbelief by future generations.

For now, however, the alimony struggle continues amidst a patchwork of confusing and often conflicting laws as couples seek economic justice. Most courts will cut through the chaotic state of current transitional alimony law and, using their broad discretionary powers, will render justice in each particular case as the facts and circumstances warrant.

AFTERWORD

The results are now in—divorce, singles bars, group sex, living together outside marriage notwithstanding—and the rages of the '60s and '70s still take second place to marriage. A look at the figures will show that the statistics for remarriage are astronomical; obviously many people are willing to try again. In a chaotic world of freedom, independence, and do-your-own-thing, many people still want their haven of security and stability—and to be "tied down." Most important, they want to share that security with just one special person.

If the specter of alimony frightens you, take a second look at your marriage. It just may be that it *could* be the best one you'll ever have—and therefore worth saving.

Appendix
MAYBE YOU SHOULD MOVE: A GUIDE TO THE ALIMONY LAWS OF THE FIFTY STATES

Each state has its own laws regarding alimony. These laws reflect the prevailing attitudes and thoughts on family and marriage held by the people within each state, as filtered through the state legislature. Opinions of alimony in Hawaii may not be the same as those in Boston or Houston. The mores of Manhattan may not jibe with the thinking in Peoria. A close look at your own community should give you some indication of how the law and your local judges view alimony. Some states use the phrase "spousal support" or some similar term instead of alimony, but this is often only a difference in labeling. In all states, judges have a great deal of discretion in awarding alimony.

The alimony laws of several states were recently held unconstitutional by a landmark decision of the United States Supreme Court, which ruled that a law which only provides alimony to a wife and not to a husband is unconstitutional. These stricken state laws have been or are in the process of being amended to comply with the constitutional requirement, that either spouse be equally entitled to alimony. In the following discussion of the alimony laws of the fifty states, any reference to "he," "she," "wife" or "husband" must be read as referring to either spouse.

The alimony laws of each state vary so much that a short trip across a state border can make a world of difference to one's legal rights. Before discussing some of the differences in the alimony laws of the fifty states, we should first note the similarities among state alimony laws.

Most states do provide for both temporary and permanent alimony. They may refer to such payments in different terms—spousal support, rehabilitative payments, maintenance payments, or alimony—but they all mean the same thing. Most states also provide for dividing a divorcing couple's property in an equitable and just manner. The majority of states recognize the validity and binding effect of separation agreements which provide for alimony. Almost all states specifically spell out that alimony payments cease upon remarriage or the death of either spouse. The great majority of states permit an alimony award to be modified when circumstances warrant. Most states also have provisions which require one spouse to pay the other a sum of money to enable that spouse to maintain or defend the matrimonial action itself. Finally, while each state has its own legal standards for determining how much alimony should be awarded, most states generally consider the following factors: the earning capacity of both spouses; their financial obligations, needs, and resources; the education and training of the parties and their ability and opportunity to secure future education and training; the standard of living established during their marriage; the length of the marriage; the monetary and nonmonetary contribution of each party to the well-being of the family; the real and personal property interests of both parties; their ages;

165

and the physical and mental conditions of the parties. Most states also have a general, catch-all standard which allows a judge to consider "any other factors necessary to consider the equities between them." Alimony awards are made at the broad discretion of the judge, so substantially different results may occur from state to state, city to city, and judge to judge.

Despite similarities among most states in their treatment of alimony, the unique provisions of several states make it impossible to make a generalization for all fifty. For example, a few states do not allow an award of permanent alimony. Texas does not permit court-ordered permanent alimony, yet Texas residents can agree to periodic alimony payments as part of their separation agreement. Pennsylvania law does not allow permanent alimony except in a case where the defendant is insane. Other states allow permanent alimony within restrictive guidelines. Colorado allows alimony only when a spouse lacks sufficient property, or is unable to secure sufficient work to maintain himself or herself, or if the spouse seeking alimony has custody of a child, making it inappropriate to seek employment. Many states, such as Louisiana, allow alimony only if the spouse seeking it has not been guilty of misconduct in the marriage. North Carolina provides that the right to receive alimony is affected if the divorce is granted upon the misconduct of the spouse seeking alimony. South Carolina will not allow alimony to an adulterous spouse. In Virginia, the spouse guilty of wrongdoing will not be able to receive permanent alimony. Kentucky law provides that while fault and misconduct are not a reason to grant alimony, it may be considered by the court in determining the amount awarded. The Ohio courts may grant alimony for a number of fault reasons, including adultery, gross neglect of duty, abandonment without good cause, ill-treatment, habitual drunkenness, and sentence to imprisonment.

Once alimony is allowed, many states handle alimony after divorce in different ways. California law creates a unique presumption that, unless otherwise agreed between the parties in writing, there is a decreased need for spousal support if the dependent ex-spouse is cohabiting with a person of the opposite sex. (This appears to be discriminatory in favor of homosexuals.) New York also has a unique and controversial provision which holds that alimony terminates if the dependent ex-spouse is living with another *and* holding herself out to the community as being married. But, if a New York ex-spouse lives with a member of the opposite sex and clearly maintains an unmarried status in the process, the former spouse will have to continue support. Under Utah law, a spouse's right to alimony is cut off if the dependent spouse cohabits with another; however, the law specifically states that cohabitation "without sexual contact" will not affect the right to alimony. What constitutes "sexual contact" may or may not be hard to prove depending on the facts of each case.

Puerto Rico revokes alimony when the divorced spouse is found guilty of "licentious behavior."

Arizona, California, Idaho, Louisiana, Nevada, New Mexico, Texas, and Washington are called community property states because they have laws which hold that all property accumulated by spouses during their marriage belong to both of them. The theory underlying these laws is that a husband and wife are "one" and form a "community." This marital community concept allows them to share equally all of the property and assets accumulated during their marriage.

And the states apply different standards in determining what happens to alimony after the divorce, too.

167

While most states allow a modification of alimony awards if circumstances change, Oklahoma does not. Oklahoma law provides that once the award is made, it is irrevocable and final. Even more interesting, Oklahoma does not automatically terminate alimony upon remarriage as do most other states. Oklahoma law provides that while alimony payments cease upon remarriage, it gives the dependent spouse up to ninety days of the remarriage to show that the alimony is still needed and not inequitable.

Oregon law makes alimony awards automatically reviewable every ten years to determine if the spousal support is still necessary and equitable. The purpose is to encourage a dependent spouse to join or return to the working world.

Various states have also grappled with the intangible in trying to evaluate work in the home. Oregon law provides that in dividing a divorcing couple's property, the court must consider homemaking as a contribution to the marital assets; however, Oregon law also creates a presumption that both spouses have equally contributed to homemaking.

Some states are more chauvinistic than others, some are more puritanical, some are more attuned to ERA, some sympathize with a wife's position and others with the husband's, and some claim alimony laws aim to support, while others claim they attempt to rehabilitate. But whatever viewpoint or approach your state takes, it is essential to consult a local attorney. Your state alimony law may be a surprise to you and may alter your view of how to approach your impending divorce. And with attitudes changing so quickly, the alimony laws of each state are under constant surveillance by lawmakers; hence, changes often occur on a yearly basis.

The following is a brief synopsis of the alimony laws in each of the fifty states. While this is intended to provide the general flavor and framework of each state's alimony laws, you must consult an attorney to know what your state law is and, more important, how that law affects your particular rights and the unique circumstances of your own case.

THE FIFTY STATES

ALABAMA—
"THE YELLOWHAMMER STATE"

Alabama provides for both temporary and permanent alimony. While divorce is pending, the court may make allowance for the support of a spouse. Upon granting the divorce, the Alabama judge may, at his discretion, award alimony if the spouse requesting support has no separate property, or if he or she isn't able to be self-supporting. Alimony may be terminated upon proof that the spouse receiving alimony has remarried or is living openly with a member of the opposite sex. The state law also provides that the court may, at its discretion, enter an order for an allowance to a spouse even if the spouse is found guilty of misconduct in the divorce. A spouse may also sue for alimony without seeking a divorce, but alimony will only be allowed at the time of or before the final divorce decree. Finally, if a spouse fails to pay alimony in accordance with the divorce decree, he or she is guilty of contempt and may be jailed.

ALASKA—"THE LAND OF THE MIDNIGHT SUN"

The Alaskan court may order one spouse to pay counsel fees to the other to prosecute or defend the action itself,

169

but there is no provision for any form of temporary alimony prior to a divorce. When divorce is granted, the court may order alimony without regard to which party is to blame for the divorce, and such an amount may be paid in either a lump sum payment or in installments. The court has the discretion to determine the amount.

ARIZONA—
"THE GRAND CANYON STATE"

The Arizona courts have power to direct payment of alimony upon dissolving a marriage. The judge may grant a maintenance order for either spouse.

ARKANSAS—"THE LAND OF
OPPORTUNITY"

Arkansas provides for temporary alimony and attorneys' fees for either party while a divorce action is pending. At the divorce proceeding itself, the court may order alimony and has the additional power of enforcing its alimony order by holding the defendant's property or securities. The court may also allow additional attorney fees for enforcement of an alimony and maintenance award.

CALIFORNIA—
"THE GOLDEN STATE"

California is often in the vanguard of developments in the law. This is reflected in its extensive alimony statutes. They provide for temporary support of a spouse while a proceeding is pending for either a legal separation or divorce. The court may order either spouse to pay the other support and maintenance, as well as the reasonable cost of maintaining or defending such a proceeding. Once the separation or divorce decree is issued, the court may order either party to pay for support of the other. The amount and length of such payments must be just and reasonable, based on the circumstances of the parties, the length of the marriage, and the ability of the supported spouse to work without hurting the children. The California law also presumes that, unless the parties agree otherwise in writing, the supported party's need for alimony decreases if he or she is cohabiting with a person of the opposite sex. Upon such a finding, the court may lower the support payment. These spousal support payments terminate upon death of either party or upon remarriage of the supported spouse. The court-ordered support payments also terminate at the end of a specified period and cannot be extended unless specified in the original court order. In enforcing its decree, the California court must first resort to earnings, income, or accumulations of either spouse, while living separate and apart from the other spouse, which would have been community property if the spouses had not been living separate and apart. Then the court can turn to community property, and quasi-community property, and finally, if necessary, to the separate property of the spouse ordered to make the support payments. California is a community property state, and upon granting a decree dissolving the marriage or legally separating the parties, the property of the spouses is divided equally, unless otherwise stipulated between the parties in writing.

COLORADO—
"THE CENTENNIAL STATE"

Colorado courts may grant either spouse an order of support and maintenance or permanent alimony without regard to marital misconduct. But it may only do so upon finding the spouse seeking the maintenance order lacks sufficient property, is unable to support himself or herself, or has custody of a child creating a situation which would make it inappropriate to seek employment. The Colorado laws also provide for temporary alimony during proceedings to dissolve the marriage or legally separate the parties. The Colorado court may also modify any award it makes for alimony if it is demonstrated that circumstances have permanently changed so substantially that the original award is unconscionable. Remarriage of the supported spouse relieves the other spouse from making any further payments. The Colorado court has discretion whether to award the alimony in a lump sum payment or in periodic payments. Colorado law also provides for a division of the spouses' property when the marriage ends, without regard to marital misconduct. The division is based upon several factors including the contribution of each spouse (and this includes contributions made as a homemaker), the value of each spouse's property including the increase or decrease in the value during marriage, and the economic circumstances of each spouse. Such a property division is discretionary with the court. Colorado recognizes the validity of a premarital agreement which says the property of each spouse shall remain separate and shall not become marital property.

CONNECTICUT—
"THE NUTMEG STATE"

Connecticut law provides for temporary orders of alimony while a divorce is pending. At the time of the divorce, Connecticut courts may assign a definite portion of either spouse's property to the other in addition to granting alimony.

DELAWARE—
"THE DIAMOND STATE"

Delaware law allows either party to request temporary alimony as the action for a divorce begins. At the time of divorce, the court may award permanent alimony to the person being sued for divorce only if the partner seeking the divorce says the marriage is irretrievably broken because of incompatibility or mental illness, and if the person being sued submits sufficient evidence of dependency on the plaintiff. Other than that one exception, alimony will not be available to the person being sued for divorce. However, the person who seeks the divorce may be awarded alimony. At the divorce proceeding, the court will also divide all the marital property of the parties without regard to marital misconduct.

DISTRICT OF COLUMBIA—
"THE NATION'S CAPITAL"

The nation's capital provides for payment of temporary alimony while a divorce suit is pending. Permanent alimony may be awarded by the court at the time of the divorce. It has no statutory provision for termination of alimony upon remarriage.

FLORIDA—
"THE SUNSHINE STATE"

The Florida law provides temporary support while the divorce is pending. At the time of divorce, alimony may be granted to either party and may be either for rehabilitative purposes or permanent. Florida law does consider the adultery of a spouse when deciding if alimony is warranted. Alimony payments may be periodic, lump sum, or both. The amount of alimony may be increased or decreased by order of the court when circumstances change.

GEORGIA— "THE EMPIRE STATE OF THE SOUTH"

Georgia has extensive alimony laws. Recent court decisions have declared unconstitutional the parts which say the obligation to pay alimony lies only with a husband.

Georgia law allows temporary alimony while a divorce is pending, and also where the parties are separated without a divorce action pending. At the time of the divorce, permanent alimony may be awarded when there is a voluntary separation or when the wife, against her will, is abandoned or driven off by her husband. But no alimony is allowed where the wife causes the marriage to end by committing adultery or desertion. If the Georgia divorce is granted on the ground that the marriage is "irretrievably broken," spousal misconduct is irrelevant to the question of alimony or division of property.

In determining the amount of alimony, the Georgia court considers all relevant financial factors including the wife's estate, her earning power, and the husband's liability to pay child support. The obligation to pay alimony ceases upon the wife's remarriage or death unless provided otherwise. Georgia law also allows a spouse to waive the right to alimony. Once alimony is set, it is subject to revision if either spouse shows a change in income or financial status. As in most states, the failure to pay alimony in Georgia constitutes grounds for contempt proceedings. To further protect a wife, Georgia law provides that when a married couple separates, a husband cannot try to cheat his wife by selling property or otherwise attempting to pass title, except to pay a legitimate pre-existing debt.

HAWAII—"THE ALOHA STATE"

Hawaiian law provides for both temporary and permanent alimony which may be granted to either a husband or a wife. The court sets the amount, and this sum may be raised or lowered later. Hawaii also provides that the decree for alimony may be modified upon remarriage of the spouse receiving support.

IDAHO—"THE GEM STATE"

The laws of Idaho allow alimony where the husband or wife is at fault for the marriage breakup. Idaho is a community property state; in the case of divorce, the court will divide the couple's property.

ILLINOIS—"THE PRAIRIE STATE"

Illinois law provides for either party to pay temporary maintenance (formerly known as temporary alimony). The law also allows one spouse to pay the other's expenses, including attorneys' fees. The Illinois court may restrain either spouse from transferring, concealing, or disposing of any property. In the divorce proceeding, the court has the power to divide the marital property without regard to marital misconduct. The court bases property division on such factors as how much each party contributed toward acquiring the property; the value of the property; the length of the marriage; the economic circumstances of each spouse; the obligations arising from prior marriages; any premarital agreement; the age, health, occupation, and needs of the parties; the custodial provisions for the children; whether the division is in lieu of or in addition to alimony; and, finally, the reasonable opportunity of each spouse to acquire future assets and income.

Illinois also provides for permanent maintenance for either spouse. To receive alimony, a spouse must prove to the court that he or she lacks sufficient property to meet reasonable needs, cannot support himself or herself through appropriate employment, or because he or she has custody of children, which makes employment unfeasible, or because he or she is otherwise without sufficient income. The court will make such a maintenance award without regard to marital misconduct. It has discretion to set the order in a specific amount for a specific period of time in light of several factors, including the financial resources of the spouse seeking maintenance, the time needed for employment training of the party seeking maintenance, the standard of living established during the marriage, the length of the marriage, age of the spouses, physical and emotional conditions of both marriage partners, and, finally, the ability of the spouse from whom maintenance is sought to meet his own needs. The parties may agree to spousal support between themselves in a separation agreement, and such a contract is binding unless the terms are unconscionable.

INDIANA—"THE HOOSIER STATE"

Indiana law allows for a provisional order for temporary maintenance and support while a divorce is pending. The courts may also grant temporary restraining orders when necessary to restrain a spouse from transferring, encumbering, concealing, or disposing of marital property. At the time of the divorce, the court must divide the couple's property based on the contribution each spouse made to the acquisition of property, the extent of acquisition prior to the marriage, the economic circumstances of the spouses, the conduct of the parties during the marriage, and the earnings or earning ability of each spouse. The parties themselves may agree in writing to spousal maintenance, and this agreement can be incorporated in the final decree of divorce.

IOWA—"THE HAWKEYE STATE"

Iowa law allows for a no-fault type of divorce in cases where the marriage has broken down to the point that the objectives of matrimony have been destroyed, and there remains no reasonable likelihood the relationship can be preserved. While the action is pending, the court may order either party to pay spousal support and fees to enable the other party to prosecute or defend the matrimonial action. The court may also attach a person's property to make such a temporary order effective. At the time of the final decree, the court may order alimony for either party, employing a general standard of what is "just."

KANSAS— "THE SUNFLOWER STATE"

The laws of Kansas have unique provisions which provide for emergency relief to protect members of a family from abusive treatment. This law provides immediate help to any family member who alleges abuse. The court may grant all kinds of relief to correct the abusive situation, including ordering support payments for the spouse. Kansas courts can also provide for temporary or permanent alimony. The court may give support to either party while the divorce is pending, and the court order directing it may be enforced by an order to garnishee wages. At the time of the final divorce decree, the court may award permanent alimony to either party in a lump sum, in periodic payments, on a percentage of earnings basis, or on any other reasonable basis. The court may also modify any alimony award. Kansas law also provides that the property of a divorcing couple may be divided. This would include property owned by either spouse prior to the marriage, acquired by either spouse in his or her own name after the marriage, or acquired by joint efforts. The court may achieve the division in any manner which is just and proper, and, if necessary, it may order a sale of the property and divide the proceeds. The parties themselves may enter into a separation agreement to divide their personal and real property and determine alimony, but such an agreement must be incorporated and confirmed in the divorce decree. The alimony and property terms of such a separation agreement are not subject to change.

KENTUCKY—
"THE BLUEGRASS STATE"

Kentucky divorces are called Dissolutions of Marriage. While an action for dissolution is pending, the law provides for temporary maintenance. The court may also temporarily order an injunction or restraining order to preserve the property rights of the spouses while the divorce is pending. At the time of the final dissolution of the marriage, permanent maintenance may be awarded. The grounds for both temporary and permanent maintenance are: insufficient property available to cover reasonable needs, inability of a spouse to be self-supporting through appropriate employment, or circumstances which make it inappropriate for a spouse with custody of a child to seek employment outside the home. The court may set the amount and length of spousal maintenance as it deems just. In making such an award, the court must consider several factors, including the separate financial resources available to the spouse seeking maintenance, the time necessary to acquire education or training for appropriate employment, the parties' former standard of living, the length of the marriage, their ages, the physical and emotional conditions of the spouse seeking maintenance, and whether the spouse from whom maintenance is sought can take care of himself if taking care of the other. While fault and misconduct are not reasons to grant spousal maintenance, the law says they may be considered by the court in determining the dollar amount.

Separation agreements between the parties are encouraged and are binding upon the Kentucky court. The court will enforce such agreements unless, after considering all the economic circumstances of the parties, it finds the provisions are unconscionable. The court may also divide the marital property of the parting couple. Fault may still be a factor in such a division. Whenever spousal maintenance is granted, the court may later modify it if one party shows that a permanent substantial change of circumstances makes the existing terms unconscionable. Finally, Kentucky law provides that, unless otherwise expressly agreed to or provided for in the decree, alimony ends with the death of either party or the remarriage of the spouse receiving maintenance.

LOUISIANA—
"THE PELICAN STATE"

Louisiana law is somewhat restrictive and will allow alimony only when the spouse seeking it is not guilty of misconduct in the marriage and does not have sufficient means for self-support. The alimony cannot exceed one third of the paying spouse's income. The law further provides that alimony will be revoked if it becomes unnecessary, and it will automatically end if the recipient remarries. A similar alimony allowance may be allowed while the divorce action is pending. Louisiana law also provides that a general or special mortgage may be recorded to secure any alimony payment ordered by the Louisiana court. These provisions for alimony may be granted in either a legal separation action or a divorce action.

MAINE—"THE PINE TREE STATE"

The Maine court may order either spouse to pay alimony or attorneys' fees to the other while the divorce action is pending. At the time of the divorce itself, the court may order alimony payments—made out of a spouse's property—to continue and may further order payment for the defense or prosecution of the matrimonial action. The law gives broad discretion to the Maine court in dealing with alimony. For instance, it may order one spouse's real estate given to the other spouse for life. The court also may order lump sum alimony in lieu of periodic payments. The Maine court may at any time alter, amend, or suspend an alimony award. However, the court may not increase an alimony award if the divorce decree itself prohibits such an increase.

The court also has strong powers to enforce payment of alimony. Upon default of an alimony payment, a criminal contempt proceeding may follow. The court may order up to ten days in jail for the first failure to pay alimony, up to thirty days for a second offense, and up to ninety days for any subsequent offense. Maine law provides that a county shall support the ex-wife and children while a defaulting husband is in jail. However, failure to pay alimony is considered criminal contempt if the ex-spouse was able to pay the alimony when it was due. The Maine court also has broad powers over the disposition of marital property. All property acquired after the marriage and before the divorce or separation is considered to be marital property unless shown otherwise.

MARYLAND—
"THE OLD LINE STATE"

Maryland law allows temporary alimony when a divorce is pending and when a spouse is in need. The Maryland court may also allow a sum for litigation expenses, including counsel fees, when his or her income is insufficient. Permanent alimony is also allowed at the time the absolute divorce or legal separation is granted, and the court may later modify that award. This right to alimony ceases on remarriage or upon the death of the paying spouse.

Maryland law also provides for a division of the spouses' property. The couple themselves may make a separation agreement covering support, maintenance, and property rights, and the contract will be binding and enforceable. But the Maryland court may modify the agreement's alimony provisions unless alimony has been waived, or if the agreement specifically provides there shall be no changes in the amount.

MASSACHUSETTS—
"THE BAY STATE"

Massachusetts law allows temporary alimony. The court may require a spouse to pay for the other spouse to maintain or defend the matrimonial action, and temporary alimony while the divorce is pending. At the time of the divorce, permanent alimony may be awarded, and the court can later change the amount and conditions. In determining the amount of alimony, the Massachusetts court must consider the length of the marriage; the conduct of the parties during the marriage; their ages, health, stations, and occupations; their incomes and the sources of it; their vocational skills and employability; their estate; the liabilities and needs of each; and their opportunities for future acquisition of capital assets and income. The court has discretion to also consider the contribution of each person in any acquisition, preservation, or increase in value of each of their respective properties, as well as the contribution of each as homemakers to their family.

The court also has power to divide the property of the spouses in addition to or in lieu of alimony, using the same factors employed to set alimony. The property of the divorcing couple is subject to this division regardless of whose name the property is held in or how it was acquired. Massachusetts law also recognizes private agreements between spouses which provide for alimony and which dispose of their property interests, if such terms are fair and entered into freely.

MICHIGAN—
"THE WOLVERINE STATE"

Michigan law provides for both temporary and permanent alimony. At the time of the divorce, the court may award permanent alimony, and the court may later alter this amount. The remarriage of the wife may be a reason for annulling any such alimony award, but it does not do so automatically. At the time of the divorce, the court will also divide the property of the spouses in an equitable manner.

MINNESOTA—
"THE NORTH STAR STATE"

Minnesota law allows a court, at its discretion, to direct payment of temporary maintenance and support while a divorce is pending. At the time of the dissolution of the marriage, the court may award alimony from the future income of one spouse to support the other. Such an order for alimony may later be modified. The court may also divide the couple's property equitably at the time of the divorce. To enforce its support orders, the court may reach the property of a nonresident defendant in a divorce proceeding, may appoint a trustee to handle the support payment, may hold (sequester) the property of the paying spouse, or may order the paying spouse's employer or trustee to withhold the alimony from earnings or trust income.

MISSISSIPPI—
"THE MAGNOLIA STATE"

Mississippi law allows temporary or permanent alimony to either the wife or husband.

MISSOURI—
"THE SHOW-ME STATE"

Missouri law allows for both temporary and permanent maintenance. The divorce decree which orders alimony may be modified only if circumstances have changed so substantially and permanently that terms of the existing support order are unreasonable. The obligation to pay alimony ends with the death of either party or upon the remarriage of the recipient, unless it is otherwise agreed to in writing or in the divorce decree. The Missouri court also has power to divide the property of a divorcing couple in a way it deems just.

MONTANA—
"THE TREASURE STATE"

Montana law provides for temporary and permanent alimony. At the time of the final divorce decree, the court may grant a permanent maintenance award for either spouse—without regard to marital misconduct. But such alimony will be awarded only if the petitioning spouse lacks property sufficient to meet needs and can't work, or if he or she can't work because there are dependents to be cared for. If circumstances change, the alimony award may be modified. If the divorce decree does not provide for alimony, an alimony award can still be made within two years. Alimony ends upon the recipient's remarriage or the death of either party.

The Montana court also has power to equitably apportion a spouse's property without regard to marital misconduct, regardless of whose name the property is in. The husband and wife may themselves enter into a separation agreement to provide for alimony, and that agreement is binding on the court unless it is unconscionable.

NEBRASKA—
"THE CORNHUSKER STATE"

In Nebraska, temporary alimony may be allowed at the discretion of the court. At the time of the divorce, the Nebraska court may order permanent alimony. The court may also require the posting of reasonable security to assure that payment is made. Alimony can be changed or revoked, but if no alimony is provided in the original divorce decree, it can't be awarded later. Unless it's specified otherwise, alimony ends upon the death of either party or upon the remarriage of the one receiving the alimony.

Nebraska courts also have the power to divide the property of the spouses. The parties themselves can enter into a written property settlement, and this agreement is binding upon the court unless found to be unconscionable. Alimony may also be ordered by the court in addition to property settlement. A judgment for unpaid alimony is like any other judgment. It can be a lien on property, but it is good only for ten years from the date the judgment is legally entered or executed or from the date of the last alimony payment.

NEVADA—"THE SILVER STATE"

Nevada law allows temporary alimony. The court may require either spouse to pay the other for support and to carry on or defend the divorce action. Permanent alimony may be granted at the time of the divorce and ends on the death of either party or upon the remarriage of the recipient. The Nevada court may also modify alimony if circumstances change.

Nevada law also provides for the division of the property of the spouses. Nevada is a community property state, and the court may dispose of this property in an equitable manner and may also set apart a portion of one person's share to care for the other. Separation agreements which settle a couple's property rights are also favorably considered and usually approved of by Nevada courts.

185

NEW HAMPSHIRE—
"THE GRANITE STATE"

New Hampshire law provides for temporary alimony. At the time of the divorce, the New Hampshire court may set a just amount for permanent alimony. The court can also compel a spouse to disclose his or her finances. If there are no minor children involved, an alimony order is effective for a maximum of three years, although it may be renewed, modified, or extended for periods of up to three years at a time. The New Hampshire court also reserves the right to modify its decree if either spouse's circumstances change.

The court may also divide property of the spouses in a just manner. To protect the spouse receiving alimony, the court may order the property of the paying spouse to be conveyed to a trustee, who will invest the money and apply the trust income for the support of the receiving spouse. In all cases where alimony is decreed, the court may require security to be given to insure payment. New Hampshire law holds invalid any private separation agreements between married parties without a legal proceeding.

NEW JERSEY—
"THE GARDEN STATE"

New Jersey law provides for both temporary and permanent alimony. New Jersey courts may award alimony to either party. In doing so, the court considers the need and financial ability of both parties and the length of the marriage. In awarding alimony, the court may take into consideration the grounds for the divorce and misconduct of the parties. Any alimony order may be revised by the court as circumstances change. Remarriage of the receiving spouse ends alimony.

In addition to alimony, the New Jersey court may divide real and personal property of the spouses in an equitable manner. New Jersey law also provides that as long as the separation agreement is fair and equitable, it will be enforced. In fact, either party may terminate a separation by requesting a resumption of the marital relationship. If the other party refuses to resume the marriage, he or she will be guilty of desertion—a ground for divorce.

NEW MEXICO—
"THE LAND OF ENCHANTMENT"

The laws of New Mexico provide for temporary alimony and also allow a court to insure that each person has enough money to efficiently prepare and present a case in the divorce action. Permanent alimony is also allowed. New Mexico law provides for enforcement of an award of alimony by attachment, garnishment, execution of a judgment, or contempt. The New Mexico court also has power to divide the property of the spouses with or without the dissolution of the marriage itself. The laws of New Mexico do not specifically provide for separation agreements, but couples commonly use them.

NEW YORK—"THE EMPIRE STATE"

In 1980 New York State drastically revised its alimony laws. An equitable distribution statute was adopted which allows judges to distribute property acquired during a marriage on what the court believes to be an equitable basis. The law also eliminates the term "alimony" and refers to support between spouses as "maintenance payments." These maintenance payments, at the court's discretion, may be available to either side for varying periods of time to enable a spouse to become self-supporting.

A maintenance payment award may be modified even on the basis of unpaid installments which have built up before the application for modification. Unlike many other states, New York law allows a defaulting spouse to erase any past payments due if the court finds one spouse unable to pay. Maintenance payments end upon death or remarriage. They may also be terminated if the receiving spouse is living with another and holding himself or herself out to the community as married to that person.

New York law also provides that maintenance payments may be suspended if the custodial parent receiving it interferes with the visitation rights of the other parent. In any support proceeding, New York requires both parties to disclose their financial status. The husband may also be required to post security for maintenance payments and upon nonpayment, his property may be sequestered in certain cases and a receiver appointed. Or, the New York court may enter a judgment against him for the amount owed or punish him in a contempt proceeding. Wage and pension attachment is also authorized in certain cases.

With the new equitable distribution law, a New York judge may consider the following ten factors when dividing property acquired during the marriage:

1) The income and property of each party at the time of marriage and at the time of the commencement of the action;

2) The length of the marriage and the age and health of both parties;

3) The need of a custodial parent to occupy or own the marital residence and to use or own its household effects;

188

4) The loss of inheritance and pension rights upon dissolution of the marriage as of the date of dissolution;

5) Any award of maintenance already made by the court;

6) Any equitable claim to, interest in, or direct or indirect contribution made to the acquisition of such marital property by the party not having title, including joint efforts or expenditures and contributions and services as a spouse, parent, wage-earner, and homemaker, and to the career or career potential of the other party;

7) Liquid or nonliquid character of all marital property;

8) The probable future financial circumstances of each party;

9) The impossibility or difficulty of evaluating any component asset or any interest in a business, corporation, or profession, and the economic desirability of retaining such asset or interest intact and free from any claim or interference by the other party; and

10) Any other factor which the court shall expressly find to be just and proper.

This new law places a great deal of discretion in the judge and provides him with a broad framework in which to divide up equitably the assets accumulated by a couple during their marriage.

NORTH CAROLINA— "THE TAR HEEL STATE"

Temporary and permanent alimony is allowed in North Carolina. Alimony may be awarded with or without a divorce. In setting alimony, the court will consider the spouses' respective property, earnings and earning capacity, physical and mental condition, standard of living to which they are both accustomed, and other relevant facts. If a divorce is granted upon the grounds of adultery of the dependent spouse, his or her right to receive alimony may be lost. Also, if the receiving spouse obtains a divorce on the ground of separation as provided by North Carolina statute, then likewise the right to receive alimony will be impaired. North Carolina law does recognize the validity of separation agreements.

NORTH DAKOTA— "THE FLICKERTAIL STATE"

The laws of North Dakota provide for temporary alimony. The court, in its discretion, may require either party to pay alimony to support the other spouse. The North Dakota court may also require either party to pay for the other to prosecute or defend the divorce action. When the divorce is granted, the court may award permanent alimony and divide the couple's property. An alimony award may be modified later. The North Dakota court may require either party to give reasonable security to assure payment of alimony and may enforce its alimony order by the appointment of a receiver or other steps.

OHIO—"THE BUCKEYE STATE"

Ohio courts may grant alimony to either party while a divorce is pending. Permanent alimony may be allowed at the time of the divorce. The court may enjoin either party from disposing of property while a proceeding to seek alimony is pending. The Ohio court may grant alimony for a number of causes, including adultery, gross neglect of duty, abandonment without good cause, ill-treatment, habitual drunkenness, or a prison sentence.

In awarding alimony, the court has power to direct that it be paid in a lump sum, in installments, or by conveyance of property.

OKLAHOMA—
"THE SOONER STATE"

Oklahoma allows temporary alimony only after the petition for divorce has been filed. The court may also order one spouse to give the other money to prepare efficiently for the matrimonial action. At the time of the divorce, permanent alimony may be awarded to either spouse and constitutes a final determination which cannot be changed. At the time of the divorce decree, the court also specifies the amount of any property settlement. The alimony payments end upon the recipient's death or his or her remarriage, unless it can be shown within ninety days of the marriage that the alimony is still needed and not inequitable.

The court may divide the couple's property even if the divorce is denied. If a divorce is granted, the spouse obtaining the decree based on the fault of the other party may have restored into his or her name all property acquired after the marriage. Oklahoma law also provides separation agreements are not binding upon the court and may be closely scrutinized to determine whether they are reasonable, fair, and just.

OREGON—"THE BEAVER STATE"

Oregon, which has a no-fault divorce law, allows both temporary and permanent alimony. Permanent alimony may be ordered at the time of the divorce in either a lump sum or in installments. The court may appoint a trustee to administer the alimony and has power to

191

change the amount of alimony later. Alimony order is based on factors including the length of the marriage, the ages of the spouses, their health, their work experience and financial resources, child custody, and the need for education or retraining to become employable. After ten years, an alimony hearing is authorized to determine whether the supported party who is still under age 60 has made reasonable efforts to become self-supporting. At that hearing, the court considers the age of the recipient; his or her health; the work experience and earning capacity of both parties; the age, health, and dependency of minor children; and the receiving spouse's efforts to improve his or her chances for employment.

Oregon law also provides for division of a couple's property when the marriage is dissolved, and the court may order a division. In making its determination, the court must consider a spouse's contribution as a homemaker as a contribution to the marital assets. Unless one spouse can demonstrate otherwise, the court presumes each spouse contributed equally as homemakers. The court also requires full disclosure of assets and may consider the tax consequences of any proposed order. Misconduct or fault in causing the marriage breakdown may not be considered by the court. Any property settlement agreement between the parties may be approved by the court.

PENNSYLVANIA— "THE KEYSTONE STATE"

Pennsylvania law provides for temporary alimony while a divorce is pending along with reasonable counsel fees and expenses. But Pennsylvania does not allow permanent alimony except in a case where the defendant was divorced while insane.

PUERTO RICO

Puerto Rico provides for temporary alimony. At the time of the divorce, permanent alimony will be awarded to the wife if the divorce is in her favor and if it is shown she does not have sufficient means to subsist. However, the court limits her alimony to a maximum one-fourth of the husband's income. This alimony can be revoked if it becomes unnecessary, if the divorced wife remarries, or if she is guilty of "licentious behavior." Puerto Rico has a community property law, and dissolution of the marriage requires a court to divide the couple's assets. Puerto Rico has no laws which recognize or enforce separation agreements.

RHODE ISLAND—"LITTLE RHODY"

Rhode Island law provides for spousal support without a divorce when either party is insane or a divorce is pending. Rhode Island Family Court has jurisdiction to order alimony and counsel fees. At the time of the divorce, the Rhode Island court may order permanent alimony. Such decrees of alimony may later be changed or annulled for cause. The award of alimony is automatically terminated by remarriage unless the divorce decree specifies otherwise. In addition to or instead of alimony, the Rhode Island court may assign either spouse a portion of the other's property.

SOUTH CAROLINA— "THE PALMETTO STATE"

The laws of South Carolina provide for both temporary and permanent alimony for nonadulterous spouses in a lump sum or in periodic payments. Where there are chil-

193

dren, support money will be allocated between the spouse and children. The court also has power to modify or terminate any alimony award. Family Court has jurisdiction to divide all of the real and personal property of the spouses in any marital litigation.

SOUTH DAKOTA— "THE COYOTE STATE"

While a divorce is pending, the South Dakota court may require one spouse to pay as alimony any money necessary to support the other spouse. The court may also require one spouse to pay to the other spouse money to prosecute or defend the marital action. After the divorce is granted, an alimony order can be changed.

The court also has power to divide the property of the spouses at the time of the divorce, whether property is in the name of one or both spouses. In dividing the property, fault or wrongdoing in the marriage will not be taken into account unless directly relevant to the acquisition of the property during the marriage. The laws of South Dakota also provide that a husband and wife may agree in writing to immediate separation and may make provision for temporary alimony during the separation.

TENNESSEE— "THE VOLUNTEER STATE"

Tennessee law provides for both temporary and permanent alimony. The amount is set at the discretion of the court, and counsel fees may be included. Permanent alimony is given only if the complainant succeeds in winning a divorce. The amount of alimony may be changed later. The court may, at its discretion, adjust the property rights and interest of the spouses in all jointly owned property regardless of whether a divorce is granted.

TEXAS—"THE LONE STAR STATE"

Temporary alimony is allowed in Texas when a spouse does not have sufficient income to survive while the divorce is pending. The Texas court may also make temporary orders respecting the couple's property. Texas is among that handful of states that do not allow court-ordered permanent alimony. However, the parties can agree to periodic alimony payments as part of a separation agreement. Such consensual alimony is enforced as a binding contract.

While the court will not order permanent alimony, it will divide a couple's property fairly, with regard for each spouse and the children. Separation agreements are recognized in Texas if the parties are actually separated at the time the agreement is made. An agreement which divides the couple's property is enforceable if it is fair.

UTAH—"THE BEEHIVE STATE"

The laws of Utah provide separate maintenance for a spouse who has been deserted or neglected by his or her mate. The court has power to assign or set apart, for the deserted or neglected spouse, alimony and use of parts of the other spouse's real and personal property or earnings. The Utah court may require temporary support and counsel fees while the divorce is pending. The court also has power to restrain a spouse from disposing of or encumbering any of his or her real estate during the pending action.

At the time of the divorce, the Utah court may

award real or personal property to a spouse and may also order alimony. Any award of alimony may be changed or terminated by the court upon proof of voluntary and permanent reconciliation. Unless the decree states otherwise, alimony automatically ends upon remarriage of the receiving spouse. An ex-spouse will also lose the right to alimony upon cohabitation, except cohabitation *without sexual contact*. What constitutes "sexual contact" is a matter of proof.

VERMONT—
"THE GREEN MOUNTAIN STATE"

Vermont law provides for temporary alimony any time the couple is separated. The court may make such an order after a hearing. The Vermont court may also allow permanent alimony to either party. It may require either party to disclose under oath what property has come to him or her by reason of the marriage in order to set the amount of alimony. The court may also change the award later. When a divorce is granted, the court may award real and personal property to either spouse.

VIRGINIA—"THE OLD DOMINION"

Virginia law provides for temporary alimony and payment to enable a spouse to conduct the divorce action. The court may also order either side not to dispose of property until the issue of support is settled. At the time of the divorce, the Virginia court may order permanent alimony to the person seeking the divorce. The person against whom the divorce was granted may also be awarded alimony, but only if the divorce was granted on the ground of separation. In other words, the one guilty of wrongdoing in the marriage will not be able to receive permanent alimony.

In awarding permanent alimony, the court will consider factors, including the earning capacity, obligations, needs and financial resources of the spouses; the education and training of the parties and their ability to get education and training; the standard of living established during the marriage; the length of the marriage; the monetary and nonmonetary contribution of each party to the well-being of the family; the real and personal property interests of both parties; their ages, and physical and mental condition. The court may award periodic payments or a lump sum support payment but has no authority to order spousal support to continue after the death of the person ordered to pay. The Virginia court may alter spousal support as long as there is no contract between the parties which prohibits such change. Unless otherwise provided in a contract, spousal support will cease upon death or remarriage. The Virginia court may also require the posting of security to insure compliance with an alimony order.

VIRGIN ISLANDS

The Virgin Islands makes no statutory provision for temporary alimony. However, the right to such support is so fundamental that the Virgin Islands recognizes it even in the absence of law. The Virgin Islands provides for permanent alimony, without regard to who was at fault for the marriage breakdown. Alimony is based on need and paid either in a lump sum or periodic installments.

There is no statutory provision for a division of a spouse's property, except that a court may order the delivery to a wife of her personal property in the possession and control of her husband, at the time of the divorce.

197

Nor is there statutory provision for separation agreements. While the court is therefore not bound to accept the judgment of the parties themselves on the question of alimony, a separation agreement may be halpful to the court in setting alimony.

WASHINGTON—
"THE EVERGREEN STATE"

While a divorce is pending, the courts of Washington may make temporary disposition of property. At the time of the divorce, the Washington court may grant alimony to either spouse without regard to marital misconduct. In making such a determination, the court will consider factors including financial resources of the parties, the time necessary for the spouse seeking maintenance to gain training for appropriate employment, the standard of living maintained during the marriage, the length of the marriage, and the age and physical and emotional condition of the spouse seeking maintenance.

The Washington court may also divide the couple's property without regard to marital misconduct. In dividing the marital property, the court will consider factors including the nature and extent of the joint and separate property, the length of the marriage, and the economic circumstances of each spouse at the time of the division of property. The parties to a marriage may also enter into a written separation agreement providing for alimony, and such a contract will be binding on the court.

WEST VIRGINIA—
"THE MOUNTAIN STATE"

West Virginia courts may, at any time after the commencement of a marital action, order either party to pay support for the other and money to enable a spouse to carry on or defend the divorce action. The court may also direct either spouse to hold onto property or savings until the case is settled and even to post security to guarantee compliance with such an order.

At the time of the divorce, the court may order alimony and can change it later. There are no statutory provisions for separation agreements in West Virginia, but they are permitted under common law.

WISCONSIN— "THE BADGER STATE"

Wisconsin law provides for both temporary and permanent alimony. The Wisconsin court or Family Court Commissioner may order either party to pay for the support of the other and money to enable a spouse to carry on or respond to a divorce action.

At the time of the divorce, the court may grant either party maintenance payments, which may be revised except where the divorce judgment specifically waived such maintenance payments. If the party receiving maintenance support payments remarries, the court must halt alimony if asked to by the one paying the support. The Wisconsin court may also divide the property of the spouses.

WYOMING— "THE EQUALITY STATE"

Both temporary and permanent alimony may be granted by Wyoming courts. The court may also make an allowance for the prosecution or defense of the divorce action. At the time the divorce is granted, the Wyoming court may order alimony and may later change the amount.

Wyoming law makes no provisions for separation agreements, but they are recognized and enforced if incorporated into the divorce decree.

The Wyoming court also has the power to divide the marital property. The court will consider which person acquired the property and the burdens imposed on the property for the benefit of either spouse or their children.

Notes

1. Kelly v. Kelly, S.C. 32 L.J. 181 (1863).
2. Romaine v. Chauncey, 129 NY 566, 29 NE 826 (1892).
3. Burr v. Burr, 7 Hill's Reports 207 (1843).
4. Orr v. Orr, 440 US 268, 995. Ct. 1102, 59 L. Ed. 2d 306 (1979).
5. In People ex rel Himber v. Himber, 136 NYS 2d 456 (1934.
6. Fuller v. Fuller, 33 Kan 582, 7 P 241 (1885).
7. Rhodes v. Stone, 17 NYS 561, 63 Hun 624 (1892).
8. Vincent v. Moriarty, 31 AD 484, 52 NYS 519 (1898).
9. Delamour v. Roger, 7 La. Ann 152 (1852).
10. Trovinger v. M'Burnery, 5 Cow. 253 (1825).
11. Bridges v. Bridges, 125 Cal APP2d 359, 270 P 2d 69 (1954).
12. Keene v. Keene, 57 Cal 2d 657, 371 P 2d 329 (1962).
13. Trutalli v. Merawglia, 215 Cal 689, 12 P 2d 430 (1932).
14. Buckley v. Buckley, 96 P 1029 (1908).
15. Vallera v. Vallera, 21 Cal2d 681, 134 P 2d 761 (1943).
16. Heaps v. Toy, 54 Cal APP2d 178, 128 P 2d 813 (1942).
17. Muller v. Sobol, 97 NYS2d, 905 (1950).
18. Jones v. Jones, 313 KY 367, 231 SW2d 15 (1950).
19. Morales v. Velez, 18 F2d 519 (1927).
20. Marvin v. Marvin, 557 P2d 106, 18 CAL3d 660, 134 Cap Rptr, 875 (1976).
21. McCall v. Frampton, 99 Misc 2d 159, 415 NYS2d 752 (1979).
22. McCullon v. McCullon, 96 Misc 2d 962.
23. Morone v. Morone, ———NY 2d———(Decided June 6, 1980).
24. Roach v. Button, Hamilton County, Tennessee Chauncery Court (Feb. 29, 1980).
25. California Superior Court, Family Law Reptr, Vol. 4, NR 34 (June 27, 1978).
26. Family Law Rptr, vol. 5, NR 36 (July 24, 1979).
27. Corbett v. Corbett, 2 W.L.R. 1306, 2 ALL E.R. 33 (P.D.A. 1970).
28. MT. v. J.T., 140 NJ Super 77, 355 A2d, 211 (1976).
29. Anonymous v. Anonymous, 67 Misc 2d, 982, 325 NYS2d 499 (Sup. Ct. 1971).
30. B. v. B., 78 Misc 2d 112, 355 NYS2d 712 (Sup. Ct. 1974).
31. Bryant v. Bryant, Maine Supreme Judicial Court (Feb 20, 1980).
32. Northrup v. Northrup, 43 NY2d 566, 402 NYS2d 997 (1978).
33. Hardwick v. Hardwick, NYLJ, March 30, 1979, Sup. Suffolk (McCarthy, J.).
34. Zipparo v. Zipparo, 2d Dept. NYLJ (May 18, 1979).

Index

Abortion, 40, 41
Adjournments, court,
  95–97, 133
Adoption, 18–19
Adultery, 2, 12, 38, 79,
  81, 123, 124
Adversary system, 84–85
Alabama, 14–15, 169
Alaska, 54–55, 169–170
Alimony: bargaining
  positions for, in court,
  87, 88–94; court
  rulings modified,
  135–137; creative
  approaches to,
  111–113; defined, 7–8;
  during separation,
  62–63; effect of death
  on payments, 103–108,
  140; effect of no-fault
divorce on, 79–83;
examples of need,
98–102; hidden assets
and, 115–125; history
of, 1–4; for husbands,
14–17, 72, 108–111;
inadequate, 102–105,
136–137; living
without, 143–146;
methods of enforcing
payment, 125–128,
130, 133–134, 135,
141–143; new
legislation on,
159–163; refusal of,
12–13, 24; refusal to
pay, 5, 12, 50–51, 93,
126, 129, 130–135,
141; remarriage and,
111, 137–141, 142;

society's changing
attitude toward, 7–9,
11, 12–13, 14–15, 39,
160–161, 162–163;
state laws on, 4–5,
14–15, 135, 139–140,
142, 159, 161, 163,
164–169; as tax
deduction, 149–151,
152–153, 155–156; *See
also* Palimony; Property
rights; individual states
Antenuptial agreements.
See Pre-marriage
contracts
Appeals Court, 105
Arizona, 78, 167, 170
Arkansas, 14, 170
Assets, hidden. *See*
Hidden assets
Attachment, 126–127

Bankruptcy, 6, 88, 142
Bar Association, 64–65
Bargaining positions, for
alimony, 87, 88–94
Bigamy, 33
Birmingham, Stephen,
56–57
Blackstone, William, 3
Business, family, 100, 148

California, 30, 32, 33, 46,
78, 167, 170–171; Lee
Marvin case in, 33–39
Chauvinism, 4, 8, 70, 71,
72, 81, 116, 162

Child support, 41, 45, 61,
81, 84, 87, 95, 109,
111, 113–114, 118,
122, 124, 125, 138;
and tax exemptions,
151–154, 155–156
Children: affected by
divorce, 21–23, 122,
123; born out of
wedlock, 13, 18–19,
28, 43; *See also* Child
support; Custody of
children
Client-lawyer relationship,
71, 74–76, 85
Colorado, 166, 171–
172
*Commentaries on the
Laws of England*
(Blackstone), 3
Connecticut, 78, 172
Contingent payment,
150
Contracts: between
unmarried couples,
29–32, 33–39, 42–43;
homosexual, 46, 50;
marriage, 26, 27; pre-
marriage, 46, 54–60;
See also Separation
agreements
Court adjournments,
95–97, 133
Court, family, 5, 43,
94–97, 114, 130, 135,
138, 142

Court rulings: on alimony
for husbands, 17, 111;
in custody disputes,
18–21; enforcement of,
126, 128, 130,
133–134, 135,
141–143; on equal
rights, 14–15, 18–19,
161–162; on gaylimony
suits, 46, 47, 51–52; on
hidden assets, 124,
126; and judges,
157–158; Lee Marvin
case, 33–39, 47;
modified, 135–137;
Peter Frampton case,
37–38; on pre-marriage
contracts, 55–57, 60;
on transsexual cases,
51–53; for unmarried
couples, 27–32, 33–39,
40–42, 43
Custody of children, 12,
61, 81, 87; awarded to
husband, 17–21, 109,
111; and Family Court,
95; in homosexual
relationships, 45; joint,
21–24; See also Child
support; Children;
Parental rights;
Visitation rights

Death, effect on alimony
payments, 103–108,
140

Delaware, 78, 173
"Disposable" marriages,
55
District of Columbia, 78,
173
Divorce: do-it-yourself,
73–74; effects on
children, 21–23, 122,
123; grounds for,
79–83; history of, 1–4;
no-fault, 77–83; rate,
55, 60, 81–82, 138;
separation and, 61–63;
society's attitude
toward, 80–81, 82, 83;
and Temporary Divorce
Insanity (TDI), 85–94
Do-it-yourself divorces,
73–74

Economy, 11, 15
Elopement, 2
England, 51, 81; early
alimony laws of,
1–3
Equal Rights Amendment
(ERA), 18, 101
Equal rights, court
rulings on, 14–15,
18–19, 161–162
Estate rights, 56, 57, 64,
86, 87, 103, 104–105,
106–108
Extramarital rela-
tionships. See Living
together; Palimony

Family, 5, 27; business,
100, 148; changing
attitudes in, 11, 17–18,
19; court, 5, 43,
94–97, 114, 130, 135,
138, 142; two-income,
8, 11, 15, 18
Fathers, unwed, 20
Fees, legal, 65, 66, 67–68,
75, 76, 155; tax
deductible, 153, 154
Filing status, 154–155
Financial disclosures,
117, 118, 121. *See also*
Hidden assets
Firms, law, 67–68
Florida, 78, 173–174
Frampton, Peter. *See*
Peter Frampton case

Garnishment, 142–143
Gay relationships. *See*
Homosexual
relationships
Gay Rights Movement,
45, 48, 49
Gaylimony suits, 45–51.
See also Homosexual
relationships
Georgia, 14, 78, 82,
174–175

Hawaii, 78, 175
Hidden assets: and
determination of
alimony, 115–125;

methods of finding,
125–128
Homosexual
relationships: attitudes
of society toward, 45,
46–47, 51; and
gaylimony suits, 45–51
Husbands: alimony for,
14–17, 72, 108–111;
changing roles of, 17,
18–19; child custody
awarded to, 17–21,
109, 111; hidden
assets, 115–125;
refusal to pay alimony,
5, 12, 93, 126, 129,
130–135, 141

Idaho, 14, 78, 167, 175
Illinois, 82, 175–176
Income, two per family, 8,
11, 15, 18. *See also*
Financial disclosures;
Hidden assets
Indiana, 78, 176–177
Inheritance rights, 28
Insanity. *See* Temporary
Divorce Insanity (TDI)
Iowa, 78, 177

*Jacqueline Bouvier
Kennedy Onassis*
(Birmingham), 56–57
Jail sentences, 134, 141,
143
Joint custody, 21–24

Judges, 157–158

Kansas, 28, 78, 177–
178
Kentucky, 33, 78, 166,
178–179

Law firms, 67–68
Lawyers: choice of,
64–72; client
relationship with, 71,
74–76, 85; interviews
with, 65; women,
70–72
Legal reference services,
64–65
Lee Marvin case, 26,
33–39, 47
Lesbian relationships, and
gaylimony suits, 46.
See also Homosexual
relationships
Living together, 13; and
continued alimony for
ex-spouse, 139–141;
court rulings on,
28–32, 33–39, 40–42,
43; vs. marriage,
25–28, 36–39, 40–42;
See also Homosexual
relationships; Palimony
Louisiana, 29–30, 78,
166, 167, 179–180

Maine, 78, 128, 180–
181

Marriage: attitude of
society toward, 10,
11–13, 17–18, 25, 26,
27, 36, 39, 83, 162;
ceremonies, 60;
"disposable," 55;
transsexual, 51–53; vs.
living together, 25–28,
36–39, 40–42
Marvin, Lee and
Michelle. See Lee
Marvin case
Maryland, 78, 181
Massachusetts, 78,
181–182
Michigan, 78, 182
Minnesota, 78, 183
Misconduct, and
awarding alimony, 79,
82, 83. See also
Adultery
Mississippi, 14, 78, 183
Missouri, 78, 183–184
Montana, 78, 184
Mortgage payments, 128,
150

National Organization for
Women (NOW),
161–162
Nebraska, 78, 184–185
Nevada, 78, 167, 185
New Hampshire, 78,
186
New Jersey, 52, 78,
186–187

New Mexico, 78, 167,
187
New York, 14, 29, 30, 31,
78, 107, 108, 126, 139,
140, 159, 160–162,
167, 187–189;
palimony cases in,
37–39; transsexual
cases in, 52–53
No-fault divorce, 77–78;
and alimony, 79–83
North Carolina, 78, 82,
166, 189–190
North Dakota, 78, 190

Ohio, 166–167, 190–191
Oklahoma, 78, 168, 191
Onassis, Aristotle and
Jackie, 56–57
Oregon, 78, 168, 191–
192
Orr versus Orr, 159
Out-of-court settlements,
85, 87

Palimony, 25–28, 40–44,
72; history of, 28–33;
Lee Marvin case, 26,
33–39, 47; Peter
Frampton case, 37–38;
See also Homosexual
relationships; Living
together
Parental rights, of unwed
fathers, 20. *See also*
Custody of children

Parental roles: changes
in, 17–20, 109–111;
single, 11
Pennsylvania, 166, 192
Peter Frampton case,
37–38
Physical appearance of
client, in courtroom,
158
Postponements, court,
95–97, 133
Pre-marriage contracts,
13, 46, 54–60; Aristotle
Onassis and Jackie,
56–57
Property rights, 13, 81,
87, 91; history of, 1,
3–4; in homosexual
relationships, 45–46,
48, 50; methods of
enforcing, 125–128,
130, 133–134, 135,
141–143; state law
and, 7–8, 42, 121–122;
taxes and, 154; for
unmarried couples, 27,
28–32, 33–39, 42–43.
See also Alimony;
individual states
Puerto Rico, 33, 82, 167,
193

Remarriage, and alimony,
111, 137–141, 142,
150
Rhode Island, 78, 193

Senior citizens,26–27, 58
Separation, 58, 61; agreements, 62–63, 104–105,
108, 132, 134, 140, 141,
147, 149, 151, 152–155
Sequestration, 126
Single parents, 11
Social Security, 27, 28, 105
Society, attitudes toward:
alimony, 7–9, 11, 12–13,
14–15, 39, 160–161,
162–163; divorce, 80–81,
82, 83; homosexuality, 45,
46–47, 51; marriage,
10, 11–13, 17–18, 25,
26, 27, 36, 39, 83, 162
South Carolina, 14, 166,
193–194
South Dakota, 14, 194
State law: alimony
requirements of, 4–5,
14–15, 135, 139–140,
142, 159, 161, 163,
164–169; and grounds
for divorce, 78, 79, 80,
82, 83; inheritance
rights, 28; property
rights, 7–8, 42, 121–122.

Tax: benefits, 27, 28, 74,
102; evasion, 118, 122,
127–128; exemptions,
and child support,
151–156; filing status,
154–155; refunds, 155
Tax deductions, 102, 119,

148; alimony as, 149–151,
152–153, 155–156
Temporary Divorce
Insanity (TDI), 85–94
Tennessee, 14, 39, 78,
194–195
Texas, 78, 166, 167, 195
Transexuals, and
alimony, 51–53

Unemployment, 108–110
United States Supreme
Court, 14–15, 159, 164
Unmarried couples. See
Living together
Utah, 167, 195–196

Vermont, 196
Virgin Islands, 78, 197
Virginia, 78, 82, 162–163,
166, 196–197
Visitation rights, 21, 45,
61, 84, 87, 95

Wage assignment, 143
Washington, 78, 82, 167, 198
Welfare, 145–146
West Virginia, 78, 198–199
Wisconsin, 78, 199
Wives: alimony refusal of,
12–13, 24; changing
roles of, 8–9, 11–13,
18, 81; working, 11,
15,108–109, 162
Women, as lawyers, 70–72
Women's Movement, 8,9,
11–12, 18, 19, 20, 31
Wyoming, 14, 78, 199–200